In association with
United Nations Children's Fund

CHILDREN
JUST LIKE ME

By
BARNABAS & ANABEL
KINDERSLEY

DORLING KINDERSLEY

London • New York • Sydney
www.dk.com

The Americas

Bolivian money

Mexican chillis

Brazilian grass skirt

THE CONTINENTS OF NORTH and South America stretch from the Canadian Arctic to Cape Horn at the southern tip of Chile. North America consists of Canada, the USA, and Mexico. There are seven countries in Central America, and thirteen in South America. The world's longest mountain chain runs down the western side of the Americas. Much of Central and South America is covered in tropical rainforest.

Alaska
Canada
Baffin Island
NORTH AMERICA
United States of America
Rockies
New York
Illinois
New Mexico
California
Mexico
CENTRAL AMERICA
River Amazon
Together, the Rockies and the Andes form the world's longest mountain chain.
SOUTH AMERICA
Bolivia
Andes
Argentina
Brazil
Cape Horn

PEOPLE OF THE AMERICAS
The first people to settle in the Americas were the Native American Indians. Today, the majority of people are descended from European and African immigrants who arrived in the Americas during the last 300 years.
The children in this section of the book come from Canada, the United States of America, Mexico, Brazil, Bolivia, and Argentina.

This 3,000-year-old sequoia tree in California, USA, is the largest living thing in the world.

DESERT MONUMENTS
In the southwestern United States there are large areas of desert. These strange rock formations in Arizona's Monument Valley (below) have been carved out by the dry desert wind.

ROCKY MOUNTAINS
The Rockies (left) run down the western side of Canada and the USA. The highest peaks rise to more than 4,300 m (14,000 ft).

AMAZING AMAZON
The Amazon rainforest (above) is the largest rainforest in the world. The huge amount of rain that falls there drains into the Amazon, the world's second longest river. The Amazon rainforest is home to half of all known plant and animal species.

FACES OF THE AMERICAS
These children come from all over the Americas.

Andrés, age nine (and Pipin the parrot), from Mexico

Gabriel, age nine, and Jamie, age seven, from Alaska, USA

Erin, age eight, from California, USA

Antonio, age eight, from Mexico

Teresita, age seven, from Mexico

Sergio, age seven, from Bolivia

8

Oscar's woollen hat is called a *lluchu*.

CHILDREN IN THE AMERICAS These are the North, Central, and South American children you will be meeting.

Oscar is from Bolivia (see pp. 10–11).

Carlitos is from Argentina (see pp. 12–13).

Celina is from Brazil (see pp. 14–15).

Omar is from Mexico (see pp. 16–17).

Carlos is from New Mexico, USA (see p. 18).

Nicole is from California, USA (see p. 19).

Taylor is from New York, USA (see p. 20).

Taryn is from Illinois, USA (see p. 21).

Gabriel is from Alaska (see p. 22).

Levi is from Canada (see p. 23).

GREAT CIVILIZATIONS
Before the Europeans arrived in Central and South America, these regions were ruled by Native American peoples, including the Incas of South America and the Mayans of Central America. These "Pre-Columbian" civilizations built great cities and monuments, such as Machu Picchu in Peru (left).

The Mayans built huge stone temples and palaces in the shape of pyramids. This pyramid, called the Pyramid of the Niches, is in Mexico.

Alligators lurk in the steamy swamps of the southeastern United States.

CARNIVAL TIME!
Rio de Janeiro in Brazil is famous for its annual carnival (right), during which people dress up in colourful costumes and dance in the streets.

Pueblo Indian vase, USA

School bus, USA

SPECTACULAR CITIES
Over the past 300 years, cities in the United States, such as New York (right) and San Francisco, have grown from small settlements into some of the largest and most spectacular cities in the world.

Baseball glove and ball, USA

Cindy, age nine, from Mexico

Lidia, age ten, (and her pet lamb), from Bolivia

Matthew, age six, from New York, USA

Cassia, age ten, from Brazil

Jane, age eight, from New York, USA

Melissa, age eight, from California, USA

Sita, age eight, from New York, USA

THE ALTIPLANO
Oscar's village, Ajllata Grande, is on a mountain plateau (a region of flat land high in the mountains). This part of Bolivia is called the Altiplano, which means "high plain". The nearest city to Oscar's village is La Paz (above), and it is nearly 4 km (2.5 miles) above sea level. The Altiplano is surrounded by the Andean mountains, which soar to more than 6 km (4 miles) high.

Romualdo, Oscar's uncle

Julia, Oscar's mother

OSCAR'S FAMILY
Oscar's mother, Julia, farms the land and looks after the home. Oscar calls her "Mama". Oscar has two brothers, Efrain and Ruben, and a sister, Lourdes. Efrain is seven years old and Ruben has grown up and lives in La Paz. Oscar's Uncle Romualdo, Aunt Basilia, and their six children live just across the road from Oscar's house. The two families eat meals and work in the fields together.

UNCLE ROM
Oscar's family
meals and to li
around the ho
keep in th

CARLITOS' HOME
Like most of the people who work at Aleluya Ranch, Carlitos' family lives in a house in the grounds. The house is built of bricks, with a corrugated iron roof. There are eight rooms, including three bedrooms and three bathrooms. Carlitos' bedroom is his favourite part of the house, because he has it all to himself. Carlitos' two elder brothers live in another house on the ranch.

Chacho, Carlitos' father

Mirta, Carlitos' mother

Marisol

Mirta usually wears jeans or *bombachas*.

Matías

Carlitos

Carlitos drinking *mate*

CARLITOS' FAMILY
Carlitos' father is called Arturo, but most people call him "Chacho". While Chacho is out on the ranch, Carlitos' mother, Mirta, looks after the home. Carlitos calls his parents "Papi" and "Mami". Carlitos' two older brothers, Marcos and Juan, are 18 and 16 years old. They work on the ranch with Chacho, rounding up cattle on horseback. The family speaks Spanish, which is Argentina's main language.

Mate leaves

DRINKING MATE
Carlitos and his family drink *mate* with their breakfast, and when friends visit. It is made from green leaves and hot water, and is popular all over Argentina. Carlitos sucks the *mate* up through a special metal straw. There are holes in the end of the straw to strain out the leaves.

Mate cup

Mate straw

Marisol is 14 years old. Her name comes from the Spanish words for "sea and sun", *mar y sol.*

AROUND ALELUYA
This is the landscape around Aleluya Ranch. There are all sorts of wild animals on the ranch, as well as the farm animals. Carlitos has seen deer, otters, armadillos, foxes, hares, and skunks. Deer are his favourite wild animals.

WHOSE DOG?
Carlitos' family has two dogs, called Rocky and Chiquito. The dog that Marisol is playing with in this photograph (left) found its way to Carlitos' house a few days ago. Nobody knows where it came from. Carlitos' father wanted to get rid of the dog, but Carlitos persuaded him to let it stay. Carlitos has always wanted a dog of his own.

Carlitos

CARLITOS IS TWELVE years old. He lives with his family on a ranch called Aleluya, in Argentina, South America. The ranch is on the Argentinian pampas, which is a vast region of grassland used mainly for cattle ranching and growing crops. The nearest town to the ranch is Tandil, which is 65 km (40 miles) away. Carlitos' father is the ranch overseer (manager), and Carlitos and his brothers and sister help their father to look after the cattle. They also help out at the ranch dairy.

This is Carlitos' youngest brother, Matías. He is six years old.

"Carlitos is the same as the English name 'Charlie'."

Carlitos

"I am really called Carlos, but everyone calls me Carlitos, which is friendlier. I help on the ranch at weekends and after school. I like rounding up the cattle on horseback with my brothers. I ride as close to the cattle as I can, and I shout at them to make them run the way I want them to go. I also know how to sow seeds and plough the land with the tractor. When I grow up, I want to be an electrician so that I can mend things. I would like to travel, because I love the world. It's a very big place. I would like to go to Brazil, which is not far from here."

Carlitos with his best friends, Marcos (on the left) and Roberto (on the right).

"In the winter it is too cold to wear alpargatas, so we wear sports shoes or wellington boots."

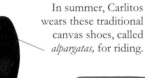

In summer, Carlitos wears these traditional canvas shoes, called *alpargatas,* for riding.

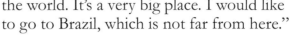

Carlitos' colourful belt is called a *faja.*

Carlitos and Matías are wearing traditional Argentinian horse-riding trousers, called *bombachas.*

This plaque shows the name of Carlitos' school, and the date on which it was founded.

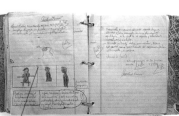

Carlitos' school

The front of Carlitos' exercise book shows a drawing of Paris, France.

"I chose this page of my natural science book to show you because it's my tidy page."

TO SCHOOL ON THE BUS
Carlitos and Matías go to school together on the bus. It takes about half an hour to get there. Carlitos' favourite lesson is social studies. He also likes playing in the playground.

"My favourite possession is my bicycle. It used to belong to my cousin, but he gave it to me when he grew too big for it. I like to cycle around the ranch, and up to the lake to go fishing. I also like playing with my model racing car."

Carlitos' model racing car

FAMILY FOOD
Carlitos and his family eat meat from the ranch every day. Their other main foods, including spaghetti, salads, and vegetables, come from the market. Carlitos' favourite meals are *milanesas,* and barbecued meat. He dislikes soup, which he thinks is tasteless.

"This is Colimba, who I ride a lot. The most exciting thing that ever happened to me was when I was given my own horse. His name is Ceniza, which means 'ash', because of his colour. He is lame at the moment, so I have left him in his field."

Milanesas (veal fried in breadcrumbs)

Argentinian sausage, called *chorizo*

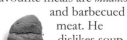

Bread rolls, called *galleta criolla*

Celina

CELINA TEMBÉ IS NINE YEARS OLD and lives in the Amazon rainforest of Brazil, South America. Celina is a Tembé Indian, and her father is the head of their village. Celina's family farms. They grow most of the food they need, and sell what is left. Her father and brother also fish in the river, and sometimes kill alligators to eat. Celina's village is very close to the Equator, so the weather is always warm, and day and night are the same length. In this part of Brazil it rains every day.

This is Celina's sister Cirleia, who is six years old.

A HOME IN THE JUNGLE
Celina's home is made of mud bricks, with a wooden roof. Celina and three of her sisters sleep in one of the two rooms, in hammocks that hang from the ceiling. Her parents and brother sleep in the other room, which is also the kitchen.

This is Muruiru Tembé, Celina's father. Celina calls him "Pai".

At night, Celina's family lights the home with this gas lamp.

Maria is Celina's mother.

CELINA'S FAMILY
Celina's family takes the name of its tribe, the Tembé, as its surname. Celina has four sisters and a brother. Her eldest sister, Socorro, is 22 years old and she is married with three children. Celina has another elder sister, Celma, who is 12 years old, and two younger sisters, Cirleia and Cintia. Celina's family speaks Portuguese, which is Brazil's main language. At school the children are learning Tembé, because the Indians want to be able to speak their own language.

Celina's youngest sister, Cintia, is three years old.

Celina's brother, Sergio, is 16 years old. He uses a bow and arrows for fishing.

Celina calls her mother "Mamãe".

AROUND SÃO PEDRO
Celina's village, São Pedro, is on the banks of the Rio Guama, which flows into the Amazon. There is no bridge at São Pedro, and the villagers cross the river by canoe. The nearest city to São Pedro is Belém, which is four hours away by road. Much of the rainforest between São Pedro and Belém has been chopped down to make way for planting crops.

WATER FROM THE WELL
Every day, Celina collects water from the village well (right). She carries it in a dried, hollowed-out *cabaça*, a type of fruit that grows in the forest nearby.

Dried *cabaça* fruit for carrying water

"I never wear a T-shirt, not even to school, because I would be too hot."

"My friend Monique trims my hair for me."

Celina paints her face and body every day.

Celina

"I am called Celina Tembé, because I am a Tembé Indian. I have just started to learn Tembé, which is our own language. I like living by the river – I want to live here for the rest of my life. I love the forest, and it makes me sad when people chop down the trees. Sometimes at night the forest scares me, because the Matim lives there. The Matim is a huge animal that grown-ups say is imaginary. I've never seen it, but I know it's there because I hear it whistling. I'm very scared of the Matim."

CELINA'S FRIENDS
Celina and her friends Anna-Paula (on the left) and Monique (on the right) like to play with dolls together.

Urucum seed pods and seeds

Seeds from the *urucum* plant are crushed to a paste to make red body paint.

TEMBÉ TRADITIONS
Like many Amazonian Indians, the Tembé are trying to stop their traditions and language from dying out. The Tembé Indians decorate their bodies with paint made from the *urucum* plant, which grows in the forest.

"I love school. I have been practising writing in my exercise book."

SÃO PEDRO SCHOOL
Celina's school is next to her house. She has only been going to school for a month, because there was no teacher at the school before then. Celina learns reading, writing, and Tembé.

Hammocks were invented by South American Indians.

DOWN AT THE RIVER
Celina washes and swims in this small stream, which is a short distance away from the main river. Celina sometimes takes the family's canoe out on the river by herself. She never paddles far from the bank. Alligators, snakes, and piranha fish live in the river, but Celina is never afraid to play there. She says the animals would not harm her.

HANGING AROUND
Celina sleeps in a hammock made from a large piece of cloth with lengths of rope at both ends. The ropes are attached to beams in the roof. If Celina gets cold in the night, she wraps a sheet around herself.

Maniva root

"We have a dog called Tuike, and we also have this puppy, which doesn't have a name yet."

"I always have bare feet – I have never had any shoes. But I hardly ever hurt my feet."

MAINLY MANIVA
Celina's family eats *xibe* with most meals. This is made from ground *maniva* roots mixed with water. With the *xibe* they usually eat fish from the river, or meat from the market. Celina also collects fruit from the forest to eat.

Celina's family grow enough *maniva* for themselves, and sell what is left.

Xibe, made from ground *maniva* root and water

15

Omar

OMAR GUERRERO SALAZAR is eight years old. He lives with his family near the town of Cancún in southeast Mexico. This region is fringed with beautiful sandy beaches lapped by warm, turquoise sea. In shallow waters, brightly coloured tropical fish swim on the coral reefs. Cancún's beautiful coastline attracts visitors from all over the world. Omar's father works in the tourist industry. He meets holidaymakers at the airport and drives them to their hotels.

MEXICAN WAVES
Cancún is situated on Mexico's Yucatán Peninsula, a piece of land that juts out into the Gulf of Mexico. Tourists began visiting Cancún about 20 years ago. Since then, modern hotels and apartments have sprung up all along the coast. Omar's family lives just outside Cancún. It takes about 20 minutes to drive to the beach.

"I love the feeling of being in the water with the fish. They are such bright colours. Yesterday I saw a fish that was completely see-through."

Omar's grandmother | Lilia, Omar's mother | Omar | Octavio | Luis Angel, Omar's father

JOINT EFFORT
Omar's father is building the family home himself. It has taken four years, and it is almost finished now. He taught Omar and Octavio how to mix cement, and they helped him to build the walls and lay the floor. The house has one large room, with areas for cooking, eating, and sleeping. The family designed the house, and Octavio and Omar each decided how one part of it should look.

Luis Angel keeps his car in the garage.

OMAR'S FAMILY
Omar calls his parents "Mami" and "Papi". He has one brother, called Octavio, who is 14 years old. While his father is out at work, his mother bakes cakes and pastries to sell. Omar often does the shopping for his parents. He goes on his bicycle, and buys meat, vegetables, milk, and tortillas (Mexican pancakes made from maize). Omar and his brother get on very well together. Omar says that they have only ever argued four times.

Omar is about to give Gertrudis her bath.

SPANISH HERITAGE
Mexico was ruled by the Spanish for 300 years, until 1821. The Spanish took their language and the Catholic religion to Mexico. Today, Spanish is Mexico's main language, and most Mexicans still follow the Catholic faith.

Gertrudis the tortoise

A VERY CLEAN TORTOISE
When Omar wakes up in the morning, the first thing he thinks about is Gertrudis, his pet tortoise. Gertrudis lives in the garden. Omar gives her a bath every day, and she loves swimming in the sink. Omar's friends sometimes come to see Gertrudis, but when they do, she always hides in the bushes.

Omar's local church is called San Francisco de Asís, which means "Saint Francis of Assisi." St. Francis is the patron saint of animals.

This is the altar in Omar's church.

Omar

"When I grow up, I want to work with computers. I will play football in my spare time, because that's my favourite game. If I could change the world in any way, I would help all the children who are abandoned by their families. I would talk to their parents, and ask them not to make their children work in the streets. They should keep them inside, give them food, and make sure that they always go to school."

Javier

OMAR'S BRAVE BEST FRIEND
Omar's best friend is called Javier Otero Pérez. He lives in the house behind Omar's. Javier and Omar protect each other when bigger boys threaten to fight them. Omar thinks that Javier is very brave.

Mask

Snorkel

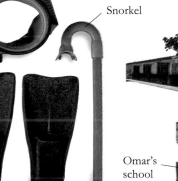
Flippers

Omar's school

SNORKELLING IN THE SEA
Omar swims in the sea almost every day. He explores the rocks and coral reefs, looking for fish and other interesting sea creatures. Omar wears a snorkel and a mask, so that he can breathe under water and see beneath the waves. He also wears flippers, which help him to glide easily through the water.

"I wear shorts most of the time. I only wear trousers when I go downtown, or maybe to a party. I like this top, because it's cool and fresh and made of cotton."

MATHS MARVEL
Omar's school is not far from his home, and he walks there in the mornings with his mother. Omar is very good at maths, which is his favourite subject. In a recent exam, he scored 96%. Omar doesn't like reading, because he thinks it is boring. He likes playtime and lunchtime best of all.

"This is my maths book. I love writing great big numbers in it."

Spicy *salsa* sauce

Chillis add heat and spice to Omar's meals.

Omar often eats refried beans with his meals.

Omar wraps his food in tortillas to make *tacos*.

TORTILLA TREATS
Omar and his family often eat *tacos*, which are tortillas filled with meat and vegetables. They also eat a lot of fruit, especially melons. Omar likes a Mexican fruit called *tuna*. It looks like a cactus, and is very sweet inside. Omar eats *tuna* with ice. It is very refreshing when the weather is hot.

Carlos

CARLOS PINO is nine years old and lives in the state of New Mexico in the southwestern United States. Carlos is an Acoma Indian, and he comes from a village in the desert called Acoma Pueblo. The village is one of the oldest settlements in the USA, and it is situated on top of a high, flat-topped rock, called a mesa. Like most Acoma Indians, Carlos' family now lives in a new village below the mesa, where it is easier to get water and electricity.

A HOUSE IN THE SKY
Acoma Pueblo is also called Sky City, because of its position high on the mesa (above). Carlos' family still has a house there. It was bought by Carlos' great-great-grandmother, who paid for it with a cow.

Laura, Carlos' mother

CARLOS' CHOICE
Carlos lives in a village called Acomita. His home is L-shaped, with a flat roof. Like many houses in New Mexico, it is made of unbaked clay brick, called adobe, and sandstone. Carlos prefers his home in Acomita to his home on the mesa, because it has a TV, a heater for cold nights, a microwave oven, and running water.

COMPUTER CRAZY
Carlos loves to play games on his mother's computer, and on this pocket computer.

"I like everything about the world except for all the wars. We are very lucky in America, because we're not at war. If I could wish for anything, it would be for peace – and to be slightly rich. When I grow up, I want to be a baseball player or an inventor. I'd invent things that don't mess up the environment."

"People call me a chatterbox, because I never stop talking."

"We have two dogs, called Skinny and Roly. This is Roly. He got his name because he is always rolling over. We never let the dogs in the house, because they would eat everything."

Jonathan
Carlos
Miah

CARLOS' FAMILY
Carlos' mother is a lawyer. His father, Manuel, is a college professor in the city of Phoenix, Arizona, which is hundreds of kilometres away. Manuel lives in Phoenix, but he returns home as often as he can. Carlos' great-grandmother lives in the house next door to Carlos'. Laura and Carlos often eat their meals at her house.

CARLOS' FRIENDS
Carlos likes his friends Jonathan and Miah because they make him laugh a lot.

Carlos catches this bus to school.

"This is my school book. I am also learning to speak my native language, Keresan."

WATCHING WORMS
Carlos' favourite lesson is science. His class has made a wormery so that they can watch worms in the soil. The children used to keep caterpillars, but they turned into butterflies and flew away.

Carlos likes to wear jeans and T-shirts in winter. In summer, when the temperature can rise to nearly 40°C (100°F), he wears shorts and vests instead.

"Fry bread" with spicy beef filling
Sweet rolls
Chillis

"I would like to visit Egypt, because I'm really interested in mummies. I'd like to visit Tokyo, too, to see what such a big city looks like."

"These basketball shoes are really expensive, so I only have one pair."

PIZZA PLEASE
Carlos eats lots of native American dishes. New Mexico is not far from Mexico, and the food there is similar to Mexican food. Carlos also eats fruit and vegetables from the garden. His favourite food is pizza.

Nicole

NICOLE MATTESON IS EIGHT years old and lives in Los Angeles, a large city in the state of California in the United States. Nicole's parents work in the film industry, in a part of Los Angeles called Hollywood. Her family lives in a house with a swimming pool. The warm climate means that Nicole can go swimming almost all year round.

" I am trying to grow out my fringe, because it keeps getting in my eyes."

FUN IN THE GARDEN
Nicole lives in a large house with four bedrooms. The pool is in the back garden, along with a tree house, a trampoline, and a wooden sweet shop and jail house for the children to play in. Nicole loves the trees and plants that grow in the garden.

Michael   Laura   Sylvia

Mikie

Nicole

Nicole's favourite toy

"I like living here in LA. Not long ago we had a big earthquake. The house shook, and it was like being on a roller-coaster ride at Disneyland. It sure made a mess — lots of dishes smashed and books fell off the shelves. We got a week off school. When I grow up, I want to be an artist because I love drawing and painting."

NICOLE'S FAMILY
Nicole calls her parents "Mom" and "Dad". Nicole's mother, Laura, is a film location manager. She travels around finding places to shoot films. Nicole's father, Michael, also works in the film industry. He is called a key grip, and he works with cameramen on film sets. While Laura and Michael are at work, their housekeeper, Sylvia, looks after Nicole and her brother, Mikie.

Nicole and her best friend, Holland, like to swim in the pool and play in the tree house together.

Nicole loves to wear summer clothes, especially shorts and T-shirts.

CANDY FOR COWBOYS
Nicole's aunt made this sweet shop for Mikie's sixth birthday party, which was a cowboy party. She painted it to look like a shop from the American Wild West.

"This is our pet dog, Boomer."

Nicole's school

SCHOOL TIME
Nicole enjoys all of her lessons at school. She likes maths, because the teacher gives the class number games to play. Nicole is in a girl's soccer team, and they practise after school.

Pizza

"I always wear tennis shoes, because they are so comfortable."

Nicole has drawn and coloured in this picture of two scarecrows in a field of pumpkins.

PIZZA'S PERFECT
Nicole's family eats all sorts of food, including lots of salad and fresh fruit. Nicole's favourite food is pizza. Her mother buys the pizza base, then they add their own pizza toppings.

19

Taylor

TAYLOR MAPPS IS SIX YEARS old and lives in New York, the largest city in the United States. His father is a lawyer, and his mother makes costumes for plays in the theatre. Taylor's family lives in an apartment in the centre of the city. When Taylor and his friends want to play outside, they go to a nearby park. They like to play basketball there.

"My baby-sitter, who looks after me when my parents go out, does my hair for me. She puts wax in it, then twists it into dreadlocks."

TALL STOREYS
New York is famous for the skyscrapers on Manhattan Island. The tallest of these are the twin towers of the World Trade Centre, which have 110 storeys each.

Raymond, Taylor's father

Linda, Taylor's mother

Taylor

"It gets cold in New York in winter. This sweater keeps me nice and warm when I play outside."

"When I grow up, I want to be a fireman. I would save people by putting out fires with a hose. If I could be anything, I would be a Power Ranger, like in the TV cartoon. I especially love travelling and making new friends in other countries. I like going on aeroplanes, to islands like Jamaica and the Bahamas."

TAYLOR'S FAMILY
Taylor's parents are called Raymond and Linda. Taylor calls his mother "Mommy" and his father "Daddy". Taylor helps his parents with the shopping and housework. He cleans his bedroom and bathroom, and takes out the rubbish.

TAYLOR'S HOME
Taylor's apartment has five rooms, including two bedrooms and two bathrooms. Taylor shares one bathroom with his father, and his mother has the other bathroom to herself. Taylor likes to sneak into his parent's bedroom and jump on their bed.

This is Taylor's bedroom. He collects stickers, which he puts on his bedroom door.

"I love to wear jeans and sneakers. I have lots of pairs of sneakers."

Taylor's favourite toy is this dinosaur, which he calls "Godzilla".

Taylor carries his lunch to school in this lunch-box.

Turkey sandwiches

Apple   Fruit juice

Taylor's school sweatshirt

GOING TO SCHOOL
Taylor enjoys going to school. He walks there in the mornings with his friends. His favourite lesson is sport, especially soccer. Taylor likes doing his homework, which is usually reading.

Taylor's school books

Taylor

Taylor often goes skating in the park.

Taryn

SEVEN-YEAR-OLD Taryn Tesdal lives on a farm near the town of Morris, Illinois. This region of the United States, called the Midwest, is very fertile, and there are many farms there. Taryn's parents both work in a local bank, and they look after the farm in their spare time. Taryn has two sisters, and her grandparents live nearby.

"I always wear my hair like this. I want to grow it long, so that I can pull it up really high."

THE PRAIRIES
This is the countryside around Taryn's farm. The land is flat, and the natural vegetation is grass. These vast, flat grasslands are called the prairies.

Cheryl, Taryn's mother

Tom, Taryn's father

Taylor

Taryn

Tory

Taryn loves collecting things. These are some of her trolls.

Taryn

"When I grow up, I want to work in the store that we go to with Mom. I would work at the front desk so I could meet lots of people. If I could wish for anything, I would like a million dollars to spend on clothes at the store. I like the world, but I wish it was cleaner. We shouldn't pollute the air because pollution kills the birds and trees."

"Roller-skating is what I like doing best of all."

TARYN'S FAMILY
Taryn calls her parents "Mom" and "Dad". Taryn's sisters, Taylor and Tory, are eleven and nine years old. Taryn's grandparents also live on a farm. Taryn sees her grandmother almost every day after school.

TARYN'S HOME
Taryn's house is built of wood, and has three storeys. Taryn shares a bedroom with Tory. They sleep in bunk beds.

Taryn's drawing of a horse

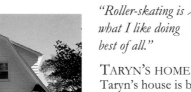

Taryn's maths book and counting sticks

Taryn's school

Taryn likes to wear leggings or jeans, with a sweatshirt.

"I usually wear tennis shoes, or slip-ons, like these."

MRS. TRUTY'S CLASS
Taryn catches the school bus at eight o'clock in the morning, and sits next to her friend Katie. There are only three people in Taryn's class. They are Taryn, Katie, and another of Taryn's friends, called Allison. Taryn likes her teacher, Mrs. Truty. She teaches them reading, writing, maths, science, and German.

"Our cats are my favourite things in the world."

Taryn's family has seven cats and six kittens.

This is the church that Taryn's family goes to on Sundays. Taryn also goes to Sunday school.

SPECIAL SPAGHETTI
Taryn's family eats a lot of fruit, vegetables, and pasta. Taryn's favourite meal is spaghetti with melted butter (right).

Gabriel

NINE-YEAR-OLD GABRIEL BRINK lives in Alaska, in northwestern North America. Gabriel is a Yu'pik Eskimo. The Yu'piks are the native people of southern Alaska and eastern Siberia, in Russia.

"Like everyone else in Bethel, I have my hair cut by Stan. He's the barber."

BETHEL
In the autumn, the rivers around Gabriel's town, which is called Bethel, begin to freeze over (above). By December the ice is so thick that people can drive their cars along the rivers.

Gabriel

"I belong to the Yu'piks, and I have a Yu'pik name, too, which is Taall'aq. When I grow up, I want to be a policeman. And I'd hunt, like my Dad. Sometimes he takes me hunting with him. He shoots moose and caribou, and birds, like duck. Once I shot a duck, but it was too small to eat."

COSY HOME
Gabriel's home (above) has two storeys, and it is built of wood. Gabriel likes his house because it is warm and cosy.

GABRIEL'S FAMILY
Gabriel's mother and father are called Marvella and William. They also have Yu'pik names, which are Akiuk'aq and Uyang'aq. Gabriel has a younger sister, called Jamie and a cousin, called Clinton. Soon Gabriel will have another brother or sister, because Marvella is expecting a baby!

Marvella   William
Clinton
Jamie

"I'd like to visit New York, to check out how big it is. I saw it in the film Home Alone 2."

Gabriel's school

"This remote-controlled car is my favourite toy. I also like playing baseball. And what I like doing best of all is eating pizza!"

SPECIAL HELPERS   My Daily Schedule

Gabriel's school book

OFF TO SCHOOL
Gabriel's favourite subject is handwriting. He also has lessons in English, maths, and Yu'pik, which is his native language. Gabriel speaks both Yu'pik and English.

ESKIMO TREATS
Gabriel's family often eats food that William has hunted, including moose and duck. For a treat, Marvella makes *agutak*, which is Eskimo ice-cream.

Agutak   Dried fish, caught by William

"In winter I love playing in the snow. We make snowmen and snow angels. Sometimes we go sledding, with a team of dogs pulling the sled."

Gabriel's boots are lined with fur to keep his feet warm.

Levi's toy cars

Levi

Levi's name is pronounced *Lee-vi*.

EIGHT-YEAR-OLD Levi Eegeesiak lives in Canada, in a remote town called Iqaluit. Levi is *Inuk* (Inuit). The Inuit are one of the indigenous peoples of northern Canada.

IQALUIT
The town of Iqaluit (above) is on the coast of Baffin Island, which lies in the Arctic Ocean. Iqaluit has snow from October until May. In winter, the sun rises above the horizon for just two hours a day.

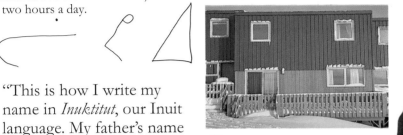

HIGHER THAN THE SNOW
Levi's house (above) is made of wood. Like all of the houses in the town, it is built on stilts to keep it above the deep winter snow. What Levi likes best about his home is the television.

"This is how I write my name in *Inuktitut*, our Inuit language. My father's name is Levi too, so I am called Levi Junior. But most people call me 'June'. The thing that I like doing best is playing ice hockey. I play for a team called The Atoms. I want to be an ice hockey player when I grow up."

Levi's parents are wearing traditional Inuit jackets, called parkas.

LEVI'S FAMILY
Levi's father is a carpenter, and his mother, Joamie, works for the government. Levi has a brother, Kipanik, who is twelve years old, and two sisters, Naiomi and Jackie, who are six and three years old. In winter, Levi's father goes hunting for caribou. He rides on a snowmobile, and attaches a trailer to the back for carrying the caribou home.

Levi   Joamie   Kipanik

Jackie   Naiomi   Levi Junior

LEVI'S LESSONS
At school (above) Levi learns maths, computing, reading, and *Inuktitut*. He speaks *Inuktitut* at school and at home, and he understands English, too. Levi's favourite lesson is maths, because he finds it easy. He thinks that reading is boring.

This is Levi's exercise book. The writing is in *Inuktitut*.

"I would love to visit Disneyland. It must be such fun there."

Levi's specially insulated boots keep his feet warm in the freezing winter temperatures.

CARIBOU AND KETCHUP
Levi often has caribou for supper. He likes to eat it with tomato ketchup. Levi's favourite food is chips.

"These are my ice hockey boots. I play forward, and I wear a black kit."

Caribou stew

Levi's doll is supposed to look like a famous ice hockey player called Brett Hull.

Greek icon

Hungarian tram

Russian telephone box

Europe

THE CONTINENT OF Europe stretches from the cold lands north of the Arctic Circle to the warm and sunny countries bordering the Mediterranean Sea. It includes the United Kingdom and Ireland to the west, and its eastern frontier runs along the Ural Mountains in Russia.

Scandinavia is made up of Norway, Sweden, and Denmark.

Finland
Germany
United Kingdom
Ireland
France
Pyrenees
Spain
Mediterranean Sea
Russia
Moscow
Poland
Prague
Hungary
Italy
Crete
Alps
Greece

PEOPLE IN EUROPE

The population of Europe numbers nearly 700 million. Europeans vary widely in appearance. Many Scandinavians have fair colouring, with blonde hair and blue eyes, while people in Mediterranean regions, such as Italy and Spain, are often olive-skinned with black or brown hair. During the 20th century, many people have migrated to Europe from other continents. The children in this section of the book come from Finland, Hungary, Poland, Russia, France, and Greece.

PATCHWORK FIELDS

Many rural parts of the United Kingdom, such as the county of Somerset (left), have small, patchwork-like fields, bordered by networks of hedgerows. Much of the countryside is very green, due to the moist climate.

FORESTS OF FIRS

A wide band of coniferous forest, called the taiga, stretches across northern Europe. Much of Sweden (left) is forested.

SUNSHINE CROPS

Mediterranean regions, such as southern Spain (right), have cool wet winters and hot dry summers. This climate is ideal for growing olives and sunflowers, two of the major crops in these areas.

FACES OF EUROPE

These children come from all over Europe.

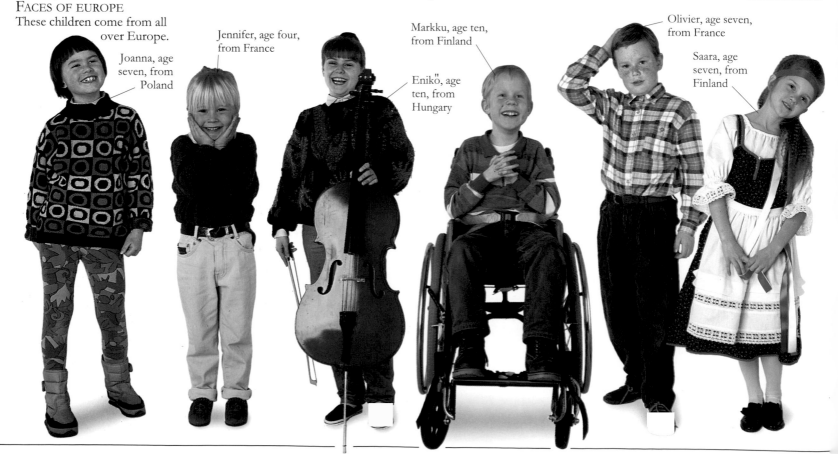

Joanna, age seven, from Poland

Jennifer, age four, from France

Markku, age ten, from Finland

Enikö, age ten, from Hungary

Olivier, age seven, from France

Saara, age seven, from Finland

CHILDREN IN EUROPE
These are the European children you will be meeting in this section of the book.

Ari is from Finland (see pp. 26).

Monika is from Hungary (see p. 27).

Bogna is from Poland (see pp. 28–9).

Olia is from Russia (see pp. 30–1).

Rachel is from France (see p. 32).

Yannis is from Greece (see p. 33).

BALLET IN EUROPE
Ballet originated in Europe and is now popular all over the world. Top European ballet companies include the Bolshoi Ballet from Russia, and the Royal Ballet from England. Many major European cities have opera houses where ballets and operas are performed.

Russian money

Mandarin, Greece

EUROPE'S MOUNTAINS
There are several high mountain ranges in Europe, including the Alps (above) and the Pyrenees. Skiing is a popular sport in Europe. In winter the Alps are criss-crossed with ski runs.

CASTLES AND KINGS
There are many castles in Europe. The first castles were built as fortresses. Some later castles, such as Neuschwanstein Castle in Germany (right), were built as grand homes for royal and noble families.

BEAUTIFUL CITIES
Many of Europe's cities, such as Paris, London, and Rome, have buildings that are hundreds of years old. Prague (above), the capital city of the Czech Republic, is famous for its beautiful architecture.

Hungarian postbox

Brown bears once roamed over most of Europe. Today they are only found in parts of Eastern Europe, and in small areas of Italy, Spain, and Norway.

Russian doll

David, age twelve, from England

Patricia, age nine, from France

Tania, age eight, from Russia

Sonia, age eight, from Russia

Yann, age five, from France

Heta, age six, from Finland

Ari

ELEVEN-YEAR-OLD ARI LAITI comes from Finland in Northern Europe. His family belongs to the Saame people, who live in the northern part of Finland, called Lapland. The Saame speak their own language, and many of them keep herds of reindeer. Ari's village, Utsjoki, is the most northern settlement in Finland. It is 500 km (310 miles) inside the Arctic Circle.

WINTER DARKNESS
In the far north of Lapland, the sun stays below the horizon from November until mid-January. These months of darkness are called *kaamos*, which means "polar night".

Selma, Ari's mother

Timo

Tero

Jouni (pronounced *Yo-nee*), Ari's father

ARI'S FAMILY
Jouni is a boat-builder, and Selma is a teacher and social worker. Ari has two older brothers, called Tero and Timo. He also has a grown-up half-brother, Toni Matti, who is a reindeer herder. The whole family joins in the reindeer round-up, which takes place every autumn. The Saame people chase their reindeer from the hills and forests using snowmobiles and helicopters. Then everyone picks out their own reindeer which they sell, or kill for food.

Ari wears his Saame national costume on special occasions.

"I don't like kaamos, because it's such a cold and gloomy time. In summer it's light all day and all night. Then I can go fishing almost every day. If I could wish for anything, it would be for lots of rivers full of fish! When I grow up, I want to be a vet. And my dream is to play for a top ice hockey team."

"Raine is my best friend because I can trust him."

Ari and his best friend, Raine, love playing ice hockey.

STEAMING IN THE SAUNA
Ari's home (above) is built of bricks. Inside, the walls are lined with wood. Like many houses in Finland, Ari's home has a sauna for taking steam baths. Ari has a sauna twice a week.

"The best thing that ever happened to me was when my uncle gave me my own fishing rod for Christmas."

ARI'S MEALS
Ari and his family often eat fish, especially salmon (left). They also eat a lot of reindeer meat.

These pages are from Ari's biology exercise book.

ARI'S SCHOOL
About 4,000 Saame people live in Finland. They want to make sure that their language doesn't die out, so lessons in some schools, including Ari's, are taught in Saame instead of Finnish. Ari can speak both Saame and Finnish. He enjoys all his lessons. They include maths, history, biology, and art.

Ari's boots are made of reindeer fur. Snow does not stick to the fur, so he can wear the boots indoors as well as outdoors.

Mónika

"I prefer playing the flute to the piano because I find it easier. I play one note at a time on the flute, but on the piano I have to play many notes at the same time."

MÓNIKA IS EIGHT YEARS old. She lives in a suburb of Budapest, the capital city of Hungary in Central Europe. Mónika's family name is Nagy (pronounced *Noyj*). Hungarians say their family name first, so Mónika is called Nagy Mónika. Mónika's father, Miklós, plays the French horn in an orchestra. The other members of the family play musical instruments, too. Mónika is learning to play the flute and the piano, and her sister, Enikö, is learning to play the cello.

Mónika

"When I grow up, I want to be a kindergarten teacher like my mother, because I think it would be nice to work with children. I'd like to visit Greece, because I could see the sea there – Hungary is surrounded by land. If I could wish for anything, I would like to have my own pet. I love Robbie the budgerigar, but he belongs to my sister."

BUDAPEST
The city of Budapest is made up of two parts, one on either side of the River Danube. On the right bank is the hilly area of Buda, and on the left bank is the low-lying area of Pest (above).

Kinga
Enikö
Miklós

MÓNIKA'S FAMILY
Mónika's mother, Kinga, is a kindergarten teacher. She used to teach the cello, and she helps Enikö with her cello practice. Kinga often takes Mónika and Enikö to hear their father play in his orchestra, which is called the Festival Orchestra. Every summer, Miklós and Kinga take the girls to stay with their grandmother, who lives in Germany.

This is Mónika's homework. She has been writing about a story that her class is reading at school.

SUNDAY SWAP
Mónika's family lives in this large block of flats. Mónika and Enikö sleep in bunk beds. Enikö usually has the top bunk, but on Sundays they swap, and Mónika sleeps on the top. So Mónika always looks forward to Sunday nights.

Mónika has been learning to play the flute for four months.

This is Mónika's sheet music. She plays these tunes on her flute.

MÓNIKA'S SCHOOL
Mónika and Enikö go to the same school. It is very close to their home, and they walk there together in the mornings. Mónika's favourite subjects are reading and maths.

Mónika's school

"This is Robbie, my sister's pet budgerigar. He can talk, but he's not very good at flying. There is a little mirror in his cage, and he likes to sit in front of it and talk to his reflection."

CHOCOLATE WITH EVERYTHING!
Mónika likes to eat muesli for breakfast, with chocolate milk poured over it. Her favourite food is crêpes (thin pancakes) with chocolate spread. Mónika's family sometimes eats traditional Hungarian goulash soup. It is made with meat and vegetables, and is seasoned with a type of pepper called paprika.

Crêpes

Goulash soup

Bogna's farm is about 80 km (50 miles) from Warsaw, Poland's capital city. Warsaw has many old buildings, including its medieval city walls (above). Bogna and her family lived in Warsaw until two years ago, when they moved to the countryside. Her mother still goes to the city every week.

Bogna

BOGNA SMUK IS TEN YEARS OLD. She lives with her family on a farm in Poland, Central Europe. The family keeps cows on the farm, and Bogna's stepfather, Peter, uses their milk for making cheese to sell. He also makes organic bread. Organic foods are produced without using chemicals. Bogna's mother, Ewa (pronounced *Eva*), is a teacher. She also works in an information centre, where she gives people advice on health issues.

Ewa, Bogna's mother

Peter, Bogna's stepfather

BOGNA'S FAMILY
While Peter looks after the farm, Ewa is busy doing all sorts of things. As well as running the home, she travels to Warsaw once a week to work in the information centre. She also teaches English in the local village (Grzybów), and helps out at Bogna's school, organizing events and trips. Bogna has three sisters. Two of them, Zuzanna and Zofia, are twins. They are five years old. Bogna's other sister, Joanna, is seven years old.

This is one of the barns on Bogna's farm.

ANIMALS EVERYWHERE
On the farm there is a herd of cows, a bull, a goat, some chickens, three dogs, and too many cats to count!

FIELDS AND FORESTS
The landscape around Bogna's farm is quite flat. It is mainly farmland, with areas of pine forest. Bogna's favourite seasons are spring and summer, because the weather is warm and the land is green. She also loves the snow in winter. Her family sometimes goes to a clearing in a nearby wood, to have snowball fights.

COLOURED CORNERS
Bogna's home is made of wood, and it is painted blue and yellow. Her parents have turned the attic in the roof of the house into a bedroom for the girls, and each sister has her own special corner. Bogna's corner is painted green, and her sisters' corners are painted red, blue, and yellow.

This is Bogna's sister Joanna. Her favourite game is hide-and-seek in the dark.

BOGNA'S CHURCH
This is the Catholic church that Bogna goes to with her family. Bogna sings in the church choir.

Bogna likes playing with her favourite cat, called Pearl.

"I feel the need to go to church, even though I sometimes get bored."

Bogna

This is Bogna. Her name is pronounced *Bog-na*.

Zofia

This dog, called Misza (pronounced *Mee-sha*), is Bogna's favourite toy.

"My name means 'God's girl'. When I grow up, I want to be a biology teacher, because then I could teach children about the environment. I think that the world is a wonderful place, but I worry about it. People don't care about nature, they only care about making lots of money. They should remember that if we destroy all the trees, then we will not survive. I get sad, too, when I hear about wars. I think it's horrible that people kill each other. I would also like to change all the gloomy grey buildings in the towns. I would make them colourful. And one more thing – I would like to travel, and meet children from all over the world."

"Ewa is one of my two best friends. I like her a lot. We tell each other all our problems."

Bogna likes playing the recorder.

Bogna's school

This is Bogna's Polish exercise book. On this page she has written about a book that she has been reading at school.

Zuzanna

The sisters wear leggings or trousers most of the time. For special occasions, such as birthday parties, they like to wear dresses or skirts.

TO SCHOOL BY "BONANZA"
Bogna's school is about 5 km (3 miles) from the farm. The local children are taken there on an old trailer pulled by a tractor. They call the trailer the "Bonanza". At school, Bogna studies biology, history, Polish, and maths. She enjoys all her lessons.

"I think that all the animals of the world are precious, even flies. Every animal has its part to play in nature."

"My hobbies are playing the recorder and the piano, dancing, singing, and making things, especially masks and puppets."

Puppet

Bogna made this witch's mask to wear in a carnival.

Peter made this organic bread.

SUPER SOUPS
Bogna's parents often make different sorts of vegetable soup for supper. Bogna's favourite is tomato soup, and her least favourite is mushroom soup. Bogna's other favourite food is pizza.

Vegetable soup

Cheese from the farm

This is Olia's icon. (Icons are religious paintings or carvings, usually on wood.) One of the figures is Olia's namesake, St. Olga.

Olia

OLIA MAIOROVA IS EIGHT YEARS old. She lives with her family in a suburb of Moscow, the capital city of Russia. Olia is training to be a ballet dancer at the Russian Classical Dance School. By the time she leaves school she will be qualified to join a professional ballet company. Olia's younger sister, Dasha, hopes to go to the same school as Olia when she is older.

THE KREMLIN
In the centre of Moscow is a large walled citadel called the Kremlin (above). Inside the Kremlin are palaces, cathedrals, museums, and gardens. The Kremlin is the seat of the Russian government.

Ekaterina (on the left) and Nikolai, Olia's parents

OLIA'S PARENTS
Olia's father works in a bank, and her mother looks after the home. In the evenings Olia's parents help Olia with her homework. They read books and play draughts with her at weekends. Olia often helps her mother with the housework. Her favourite task is vacuuming.

HIGH-RISE HOME
Olia lives in a flat on the third floor of this tall block (right). Olia and Dasha share a bedroom. Like most Russians, they take the sheets off their beds every morning and store the bed linen away during the daytime. Then they make up the beds again at night.

BEAUTIFUL CHURCHES
Russian Orthodox churches often have onion-shaped domes, and they are very ornate (highly decorated) inside. Olia goes to this church, which is near to her school, on Saturdays or Sundays, and on religious holidays.

TO SCHOOL BY METRO
This is Olia's school, the Russian Classical Dance School. Olia travels to school with her mother on the underground railway, which is called the Metro. It takes them 45 minutes to get there. In the morning Olia learns maths, Russian, English, French, and art. Then she has ballet lessons all afternoon.

The Russian alphabet is called the Cyrillic alphabet.

Olia's English workbook

English II
Work book

BLINY ARE BEST
Olia's favourite meal is pancakes, which are called *bliny*. Her least favourite food is cabbage. Olia likes to drink tea with her meals.

Tea

Bliny with sour cream

"I like to wear my hair loose, like this. But I have to wear it in a bun for my ballet classes."

Olia's mother made this leotard.

Olia's ballet shoes are made of cloth. She wears them out very quickly, and has to have a new pair every two weeks.

"I wear my leotard for my ballet classes. But what I'd really like to wear is a tutu."

"I love to wear dresses. I don't like jeans, trousers, or leggings, and I hate wearing thick woollen tights."

"It gets very cold in Moscow in winter. There is often lots of snow. When I go outside, I wear a sheepskin coat and high boots to keep me warm."

Olia's name is pronounced *Oh-lee-ah*.

Olia has written her name using the Russian Cyrillic alphabet.

"My name is really Olga, but everyone calls me Olia. I have always wanted to be a ballet dancer. My greatest wish is to dance the part of Masha, the little girl in *The Nutcracker*. I would also love to be one of the swans in *Swan Lake*. Last year our school performed *The Nutcracker* for the public, and I danced the part of a doll. We did about 13 performances. I was nervous the first time, but after that I really enjoyed it."

Olia with her best friend, Julia

"Julia is in the same class as me at school. We like to play 'mothers and daughters', and we rehearse our ballet classes together. Often we just talk, mainly about ballet, and sometimes about our favourite foods. Julia was in The Nutcracker, *too."*

PARTOS THE DOG
Russians celebrate Christmas Day on 7 January, and they give each other presents on New Year's Day, which is 1 January. Late at night on New Year's Eve, a legendary person called Father Frost brings presents for Russian children. This year, Olia was given Partos the dog. He is her favourite toy.

Olia enjoys painting pictures. She copied this painting from a book of fairy tales.

"This is my little sister, Dasha. Our favourite game is 'mothers and daughters'. We take it in turns to be the mother. Sometimes we share our toys, and sometimes we argue over them."

Dasha is five years old.

VINES AND WINES
Neat rows of vines cover the rolling hillsides and valleys around Rachel's home. This region of France is one of the most famous wine-producing areas in the world. Many wines, like those produced by Rachel's family, are named after the châteaux where they are produced. Rachel's family produces a wine called *Château Peybonhomme*.

Rachel

RACHEL HUBERT IS NINE years old and comes from France in Western Europe. Rachel lives in a region called Bordelais, in a château (a castle) which has been in her family since 1715. The château is surrounded by vineyards. The family harvests grapes from the vineyards, and uses them to produce wine.

Rachel's name is pronounced *Ra-shell*.

"I would like to have long hair, but Papa prefers me to wear it short."

"One thing that I have always wanted to do is to swim with dolphins."

Rachel

"When I grow up, I'd like to be a model or a singer. I love music, especially rock and jazz. I enjoy gymnastics too, and I'd like to enter competitions when I get older. Then I could perform in a big stadium in front of lots of people. If I won, I'd climb up on to the podium to get my medal."

"I like wearing jewellery. I bought two of my rings with my pocket money."

"I would like to wear my jewellery to school, but Maman always says, 'Take that off, it's not suitable for school!'"

Rachel   Catherine
Jean-Luc

Guillaume

RACHEL'S FAMILY
Rachel's parents are called Jean-Luc and Catherine. Rachel calls them "Papa" and "Maman". Rachel has one brother, Guillaume, who is 14 years old. All of the family helps with the wine business. When guests come to the château to buy wine, Rachel likes to hand out the wine glasses and pour different wines for people to taste.

These two bottles of *Château Peybonhomme* were produced in 1944 (above left) and 1990 (left). The year in which a wine is produced is called its vintage.

CHÂTEAU PEYBONHOMME
Rachel's home is very old, and for the past four years the family has been repairing and redecorating the 16 rooms. Rachel has her own bedroom, and she has covered its walls with posters of cats, which are her favourite animals.

Rachel's favourite meal is duck. She always has a salad with her evening meals.

Rachel's geography school book

"This doll is my favourite toy. She belonged to my great-grandmother, so she is very old. Her head is made of porcelain."

Rachel was awarded this diploma when she took part in a painting exhibition. Her painting was of a boat on a lake (right).

QUIET PLEASE!
Rachel goes to school on Mondays, Tuesdays, Wednesday mornings, Thursdays, and Fridays. She studies maths, French, geography, history, biology, science, art, and sport. Rachel's favourite subjects are history and maths. She doesn't like practical science and technology classes, because she thinks that they are too noisy.

Yannis

"I wear my hair in a style called 'the hat'. It is long on top and short at the sides."

"My little brother, Sotiris, is 14 months old. He is learning how to walk. I pick him up when he falls over."

SIX-YEAR-OLD Yannis Karagiannakis lives on the Greek island of Crete, in a town called Haniá. His father, Michaelis, is a fisherman. While Michaelis is out fishing, Yannis' mother, Constantina, looks after the home and family.

HANIÁ'S HARBOUR
The town of Haniá is more than 1,000 years old. It is built around a beautiful harbour (above), where Michaelis moors his fishing boat.

Irene   Michaelis   Constantina

Γιάννης

"My name, Yannis, is short for Ioannis. This is how I write Ioannis in Greek. I am named after one of Christ's apostles – Ioannis is Greek for 'John'. When I grow up, I would like to go to the Naval Academy and learn to be a naval officer. And I would love to visit Athens, the capital of Greece. There must be lots of toys there."

FISHY BUSINESS
Yannis calls his mother and father "Mama" and "Baba". Yannis' grandmother, Irene, often comes to stay with the family. Yannis calls her "Yaya". Yannis likes helping his father to prepare his fishing nets and lines. He puts bait on the fishing hooks to attract the fish.

Yannis' school

Yannis' Greek exercise book

YANNIS' HOME
Yannis lives in a one-storey house built of stone (above). At the back of the house there is a courtyard where rose and jasmine bushes grow. There are lemon and mandarin trees, and a large grapevine which shades the courtyard from the hot summer sunshine.

A mandarin from the tree

SCHOOL TIME
At school, Yannis likes reading, drawing, and grammar. He also studies maths, Greek, sport, and music. At playtime the children play hide-and-seek and football.

GREEK FAVOURITE
Yannis' favourite meal is a Greek dish called *souvlaki*, which is made from pieces of meat grilled on a skewer.

Souvlaki with ham, cheese, and Greek pitta bread

Yannis is a Christian. He goes to this Greek Orthodox Church, which is called Saint Constantinos.

Moroccan
postbox

Fish and
tomatoes,
Ghana

Tanzanian
money

Africa

AFRICA IS THE SECOND largest of
the world's continents. This vast
land has many deserts where it
hardly ever rains, as well as great
forests where it rains and thunders
every day. Huge crocodiles swim in
the Nile, which is the longest river
in the world, and herds of
elephants, giraffes, and zebras roam
the tropical grasslands. There are 52
countries in Africa.

Morocco · Sahara desert · Egypt · River Nile · Ethiopia · Ghana · River Congo · Tanzania · Botswana

PEOPLE IN AFRICA
Many African people live
in traditional communities
that have followed the
same lifestyles for
thousands of years. Others
live in cities, or in farming
communities. The
children in this section of
the book come from all
over Africa and have
different ways of life. They
live in Egypt, Botswana,
Ghana, Morocco,
Tanzania, and Ethiopia.

Large, colourful
butterflies live in
Africa's equatorial
rainforest.

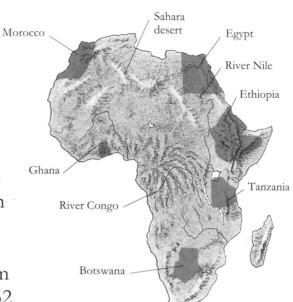

SAHARA DESERT
The Sahara (left) is the
world's largest desert,
covering almost a third
of Africa. Temperatures
in this harsh landscape
can soar to more than
50°C (120°F).

ANCIENT EGYPT
Thousands of years
ago in Africa, the
ancient Egyptians
built huge
monuments, such as
the Great Sphinx and
the pyramids (above).

FACES OF AFRICA
These children come
from all over the
African continent.

Amr, age nine,
from Egypt

Yapoyo, age
seven, from
Tanzania

Dina, age eleven,
from Egypt

Meenat-
Allah, age
one,
from
Egypt

Tshegofatso,
age eight, from
Botswana

Boitshwaro,
age eleven,
from Botswana

Hana, age
nine, from
Ethiopia

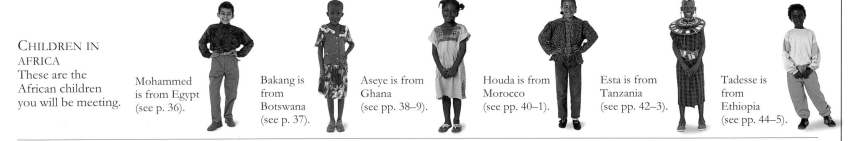

CHILDREN IN AFRICA
These are the African children you will be meeting.

Mohammed is from Egypt (see p. 36).

Bakang is from Botswana (see p. 37).

Aseye is from Ghana (see pp. 38–9).

Houda is from Morocco (see pp. 40–1).

Esta is from Tanzania (see pp. 42–3).

Tadesse is from Ethiopia (see pp. 44–5).

SCAVENGERS FROM THE SKY
Vultures (left) soar and glide in the African skies, searching the ground below for a meal. They feed on the remains of dead animals.

TROPICAL GRASSLANDS
The grassy plains of Africa (below) are called the savannah. They are home to an amazing array of wildlife, including huge herds of wildebeest and zebra that migrate great distances every year in search of fresh grass to eat. The savannah is dotted with trees that provide animals with shade from the hot African sun.

Plantains

Taxi, Ghana

Ethiopian bus

Moroccan basket

EQUATORIAL RAINFORESTS
Africa has vast areas of dense rainforest where tall trees form a canopy, and little sunlight reaches the shady ground below. In these forests, which lie on and near to the Equator, it is always hot and wet. Forest tribes, such as the Pygmies, live by hunting animals and gathering fruit and nuts.

RAINFOREST RIVER
The River Congo (left) sweeps through the rainforests of Central Africa. It eventually reaches the Atlantic Ocean after a journey of more than 4,000 km (2,500 miles). Gorillas and chimpanzees live in the forest, as well as exotic birds and brightly coloured insects.

AFRICAN GIANTS
African elephants (above) are the largest land animals in the world, weighing up to six tonnes. They live in many African countries, including Tanzania and Botswana. In recent years, many elephants have been killed for their tusks.

BIG CATS
Lions (right) stalk their prey in the grasses of the African savannah. They live in large groups, called prides.

Dina, age ten, from Egypt

Nicodemu, age eight, from Tanzania

Tumaini, age fifteen, from Tanzania

Iman, age eight, from Morocco

Zenebech, age nine, from Ethiopia

Adissu, age twelve, from Ethiopia

Mohammed

MOHAMMED ABDALLAH IS NINE years old and lives with his family in Cairo, Egypt's bustling capital city. Like most people in Egypt, Mohammed's family is Muslim. Mohammed's father works in an office, while his mother looks after the home and family.

THE PYRAMIDS
Thousands of years ago, the ancient Egyptians built huge pyramids as tombs for their pharaohs (kings). This pyramid is at a place called Giza, which is close to Cairo.

Olfat, Mohammed's mother

Ahmed, Mohammed's father

"*My most treasured possession is this football that Baba gave me.*"

"This is how I write my name. It is written in the Arabic script. I am named after the prophet, Mohammed, and my surname means 'Slave of God'. When I grow up, I want to be a policeman, because then I will be able to look after my country. I would like to travel all over the world and visit all the interesting places."

MOHAMMED'S FAMILY
Mohammed's father is called Ahmed, and his mother is Olfat. Mohammed calls his parents "Baba" and "Mama". He has a little brother called Emad, and a little sister, called Meenat-Allah.

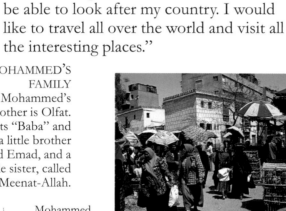

Mohammed sees this mosque when he visits the centre of Cairo.

THE MARKET
This busy market is close to Mohammed's home. People sell their goods in the streets, shading them from the fierce sunshine with brightly coloured umbrellas. Mohammed likes Cairo, but wishes there wasn't so much traffic. He says that with less traffic, there would be less dirt and pollution.

AT SCHOOL
Mohammed learns social studies, classical Arabic, English, and maths. People in Egypt write classical Arabic, but the Arabic that they speak is a little different.

This is Mohammed's Arabic comprehension book.

Mohammed

Koshari

MOHAMMED'S MEALS
Mohammed often eats a traditional Egyptian meal, called *koshari*. It is made from rice, noodles, tomato sauce, and onions. Mohammed's favourite food is strawberries.

This is Mohammed's best friend, Mahmood.

This is Meenat-Allah. She is only one year old.

Bakang

BAKANG GABANKALAFE IS EIGHT years old. She lives with her family in a village called Tshabong in Botswana, southern Africa. Bakang has lived in the village all her life. It is in a remote region, on the edge of the Kalahari Desert. The days are hot, dry, and dusty, and nights can be very cold.

"My hair is short. My sister Keoshebile cuts it for me."

"I love singing hymns at church. I call them Sunday songs."

"My name means 'Praise'. When I grow up, I want to be a nurse. I would like to get married and live in a big house, and I want two children, a boy and a girl. Every day I go with my mother to fetch water. On the way I watch out for camels because they frighten me."

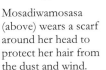

Mosadiwamosasa (above) wears a scarf around her head to protect her hair from the dust and wind.

BAKANG'S FAMILY
Bakang's father, Piet, is a cattle herder. Her mother, Mosadiwamosasa, collects wood for the fire, water for drinking and washing, and cow dung for repairing the home.

This is Bakang with her best friend Kaelo (in the middle) and her niece, Koeagile (on the right).

BAKANG'S HOME
Bakang's family and close relatives live in a group of houses made of soil and dried cow dung, with thatched (dried grass) roofs. Five people live in Bakang's home. They are Bakang, her mother, her sisters Keoshebile and Obitseng, and her niece, Koeagile. The houses have no electricity, and at night they are lit by paraffin lamps. Bakang says that her home is beautiful.

In this exercise book, Bakang has been writing words in Setswana, which is the main language of Botswana. At home she speaks Sengologa, which is the language of her tribe, the Bangologa.

Beef stew with dried spinach and porridge

BAKANG'S FOOD
Few plants can survive in the desert, so Bakang's family cannot grow crops. They buy all their food in Tshabong. Bakang's favourite meal is meat and rice. The family also eats a lot of mealie meal, which is a porridge made from maize.

BAKANG'S SCHOOL
Bakang likes going to school, because she sees all her friends there. The school is about three quarters of a kilometre (half a mile) away, and she walks there and back. At school the children learn reading, writing, and maths.

"This is my favourite dress. I wear it to church on Sundays, and sometimes to school."

"I always wear shoes to school, but at home I prefer bare feet."

Aseye

ASEYE RENATE AHADZIE IS seven years old and lives in Accra, the big and busy capital city of Ghana, West Africa. Accra is on the coast, and it is very warm all year round. Aseye lives with her mother, father, and two sisters in a flat in the city. Her father, William, works for the government in the Ministry of Education. He also has a Ghanaian name, Kofi. Aseye's mother, Sika, is a teacher at the Institute of Journalism. She also runs a shop in the evenings.

"I would like to go to London in England. It is cold there, and it snows. I have never seen snow."

HOMES IN GHANA
This is the house of Aseye's uncle. Many people in Ghana live in houses like this one, made from cement with a tin roof. Aseye lives in a block of flats. She likes it because it is neat and quiet. Her family has a television, and Aseye's favourite film is the musical *The Sound of Music*.

William   Sika

Fiam

Aseye

ASEYE'S FAMILY
This is Aseye's father, William, and her mother, Sika. Aseye has two sisters, called Fiam and Yena. Fiam is eleven, and Yena is four. Aseye often helps her mother at home and in the shop. Her family doesn't have any pets, but Aseye would love to have a cat and a puppy.

Brightly coloured plants like this acacia grow in Ghana's tropical climate.

"This is my little sister, Yena. Sometimes I weave her hair. She is wearing her favourite red spotted dress."

ASEYE'S CHURCH
Like most people in Ghana, Aseye is a Christian, and this is the church that she goes to with her family. She loves to sing hymns, and believes that when she dies her soul will rise to Heaven.

SIKA'S SHOP
This is the shop that Aseye's mother runs. She opens it in the evenings, after she comes home from work. It sells food and household goods.

Aseye

Aseye's name is pronounced *A-say-yay*.

"My name, Aseye, means 'Rejoice'. If I could wish for something, it would be that I was grown-up. I want to be a doctor, and I like learning about the body in life skills at school. Also when I grow up I would like to marry a rich and handsome man. I think that the world is growing well, but I wish it was a bit cleaner."

"Some wild animals scare me, like elephants. They could easily step on you, and then you'd be flat."

ASEYE'S SCHOOL
Aseye likes going to school because she finds the work interesting. Her parents drive her there in their car. Her favourite subjects are life skills (learning about the body), drawing, and writing. She wears a brown and yellow school uniform, and training shoes. Her best friend, Naaku Allotey, is on the left in this picture. They like to play clapping games together.

This is Aseye's exercise book. She has been writing her French lesson in it.

Aseye's favourite toy is this doll, called Maetta. One of Aseye's favourite books is *The Town Mouse and the Country Mouse*.

"This is my cousin Sesi. He is only two years old. His father is a potter."

This vegetable is a type of spinach. Ghanaians mix the leaves with palm nut oil to make a sauce called *kontonmire*. Aseye's family often eats *kontonmire* with boiled plantains.

ASEYE'S FOOD
Aseye's favourite food is called *banku*, made from corn dough and cassava (a type of plant root). She also eats lots of fried and boiled plantains, rice, fish, and groundnuts. She says that mixed vegetables tickle her throat!

Plate of mixed vegetables

Plantains are similar to bananas, but less sweet.

ASEYE'S UNCLE
Aseye's Uncle Peter (on the right) is a potter. He moulds pots from soft clay, then fires them in a special oven, called a kiln, to make them hard. Peter's son, Sesi, is Aseye's cousin.

Houda

HOUDA ELAZHAR IS TEN YEARS old and lives with her family in Morocco, northwest Africa. She lives in the town of Salé, which is on the coast overlooking the Atlantic Ocean. Salé is just outside Morocco's capital, Rabat, and Houda's family lives in the old walled citadel (fortress), called the *médina*. Her father works for the Moroccan government, and her mother is a housewife. Houda's family is Muslim; Islam is Morocco's main religion.

HOUDA'S HOME
Houda's family lives in a traditional Moroccan-style house. The rooms are built around a large courtyard, which has patterned tiles on the walls and floor. Decorated archways around the courtyard lead to the rooms, which are on several floors. The courtyard is Houda's favourite part of the house.

Sellamia, Houda's mother

Ahmed, Houda's father

Like most Muslim women, Sellamia leaves her head uncovered in the home, and covers her head when she goes outside.

Sellamia is wearing traditional Moroccan clothes. Her long robe is called a kaftan.

This kaftan has embroidery around the neck and cuffs.

These slipper-like shoes are called *babouches*.

HOUDA'S FAMILY
Houda's father is called Ahmed, and her mother is Sellamia. Houda has two brothers, Younés and Ayoub, and two sisters, Fatema and Iman. Houda's parents often wear traditional Moroccan clothes. The children usually wear jeans and shirts.

Fatema is 12 years old.

Younés is 15 years old.

This fine, lace-like decoration is often seen in Moorish architecture (the traditional Moroccan style).

THE MOSQUE
This is the entrance to the mosque where Houda's family goes to worship. Muslims pray five times a day, either at home or in a mosque, and most go to a mosque on Fridays, when special prayers are held. The holy book of the Muslims is called the *Qur'an* (Koran). Muslims believe that it contains the word of Allah (God in Arabic), as revealed to the prophet Mohammed who first spread the faith of Islam.

SALÉ
This is a view across the flat rooftops of Salé. The houses are painted white to reflect the hot sunshine, keeping them cool inside. Narrow streets and alleyways run between the houses. Salé is very old. There has been a town here ever since Roman times.

Houda's little sister, Iman, is seven years old.

"Iman is wearing her favourite pink dress. My father chooses and buys all our clothes."

"Iman's shoes are almost the same as mine."

"My mother does my hair for me. Today I am wearing it pulled back."

Houda's name is pronounced *Hood-ah*.

"This is my name, Houda, written in the Arabic script. It means 'guidance'. I like everything about Morocco, especially the seaside and the mountains. The weather is always nice here. There are four seasons, but winter is not cold like it is in many countries. I want to teach Arabic when I grow up, and I want to marry someone who likes studying, as I do. I would like to have just one child. I see on television that there is a lot of war and fighting in the world, and I wish that it would end and that the world could be peaceful".

These are some of the floor tiles in Houda's house. Moroccan buildings often have tiled walls and floors.

This is Houda's school exercise book. The writing on the pages is in the Arabic script, which Houda is learning to write.

HOUDA'S SCHOOL

At Houda's school the children play in a large courtyard where lots of flowers grow. Houda learns Arabic, French (which is spoken by many people in Morocco), reading, grammar, maths, and religion. Houda doesn't like learning grammar. Her favourite subject is reading, because she likes good stories.

"This yellow and black jacket is my favourite thing to wear."

Moroccan cooking pot, called a *tajine*

FOOD IN MOROCCO

Houda's family often eats *tajine*, which is made from meat or fish and vegetables. *Tajine* is named after the earthenware pot in which it is cooked. Houda's favourite meal is chicken and chips, and Houda sometimes cooks the chips herself.

"My little brother, Ayoub, is two years old."

These little Moroccan cakes are called *mille troues*, which is French for "a thousand holes". This is a good name, because the cakes are are full of holes.

Houda's mother uses mint leaves to make mint tea.

Moroccan snacks

Esta

ESTA IS 12 YEARS OLD and belongs to the Maasai people of East Africa. She lives at a place called Sanya Station in Tanzania. Traditionally, the Maasai are nomads, moving from place to place in search of fresh grass for their cattle. Today, many Maasai, like Esta's family, are settling in permanent homes.

SANYA STATION
This is what the landscape around Sanya Station looks like. The grassy savannah is full of all kinds of wildlife, including lions, leopards, elephants, and rhinoceroses. In the background is Mount Kilimanjaro, which is Africa's highest mountain.

ESTA'S HOME
Maasai communities live in a group of huts called an *enyang'*, which means "homestead". The huts are usually built in a circle, with space in the middle for the animals. Esta's family has ten cows, as well as goats, sheep, and donkeys. Esta's hut is made from wooden poles covered with dried cow dung, with a grass roof.

This is Esta's younger sister, Lydia.

Young Maasai children have the top part of their ears pierced, as well as their earlobes. Lydia has threaded these earrings through the tops of her ears.

Lydia wears a small necklace because she is young.

ESTA'S FAMILY
Most Maasai men have more than one wife. Esta's father, Ngidaha, has two wives. Her mother, Swelali, lives in one hut with her children. Her father's other wife, Veronica, lives in another hut with her children. Esta has two brothers and a sister, and several half-brothers and half-sisters. Her father looks after the animals, and her mother collects firewood and water, and looks after the home.

This is Esta's mother, Swelali. Esta calls her "Mama".

The Maasai wear brightly coloured pieces of cloth, called *rubeka*.

Maasai men and women wear bracelets.

Esta's father, Ngidaha, carries a brush made from animal hair for swatting away flies. He also carries a short staff to show that he is an elder.

The Maasai make their own sandals, called *namuka*.

This is Ngidaha's other wife, Veronica. Esta calls her "Mama", too.

Tumaini's special headdress shows that she is old enough to marry.

Esta

Esta's half-sister Tumaini is fifteen.

Yapoyo, another of Esta's half-sisters, is seven.

Esta's youngest brother, Daniel, is five years old.

ESTA'S CHURCH
Esta is a Christian, and she goes to this church every Sunday with her family. The church is at Sanya Station, close to Esta's *enyang'*.

It is a Maasai tradition that girls and women have their heads shaved. Esta's head was shaved by her mother this morning.

Each of Esta's colourful necklaces is made from hundreds of beads.

"I am afraid of lions. I have never seen one, but I have heard a lot about them."

"I wear school uniform to school, then when I come home I change into my rubeka. *Although the* rubeka *is comfortable, I prefer my school uniform because I think it is beautiful."*

Esta

"Esta is my Christian name, but my family often calls me Neng'otonye, which means 'girl child who is loved most by her parents'. When I grow up, I want to be a teacher. I would like to get married and have five children. I am always laughing because I am always happy. But I don't like going to fetch the water every day. We have to walk six kilometres. Sometimes there is a drought, and then the water is bad. I hate drought because the things that you plant die."

ESTA'S FRIENDS
These are some of Esta's friends. Her best friend, Manka, is second from the left. Esta likes Manka because she shares things with her. Sometimes they go together to the sweet shop, which is near the *enyang'*. They always share their sweets.

ESTA'S SCHOOL
Esta learns maths and writing at school. The teachers speak to the pupils in Swahili, which is the main language of Tanzania. At home Esta speaks Maasai, which is the language of her people. Esta walks to the school, which is about one kilometre (half a mile) away.

"These are my school books. You can see that we have been learning Swahili."

BEAD NECKLACES
Maasai women and girls wear colourful bead necklaces. The kind of necklace they wear depends on how old they are.

TOYS AND GAMES
Esta makes toys and models to play with out of the soft clay soil. She also likes to play "catch". She makes a ball by wrapping grass around a wild tomato.

Engurma is a stiff porridge made from maize.

Beans

ESTA'S FOOD
Esta and her family eat their meals with her father's other wife and children. They often eat a stiff porridge, called *engurma*, which is one of the main foods eaten in East Africa. They also eat meat and beans, and drink milk from their cattle.

This is Esta eating porridge at school.

Esta wears plimsolls to school and church. The rest of the time she wears flip-flops.

Tadesse

TADESSE ASSEFA IS NINE YEARS old and lives in Addis Ababa, the capital city of Ethiopia, northeast Africa. Tadesse's father is dead, and his mother is not well enough to look after the family, so Tadesse and three of his four sisters live at an orphanage in the city. The orphanage is run by a woman called Abebech Gobena, who founded it in 1980. That year, Abebech left her own home to look after 21 children who were victims of a famine in Ethiopia. Now there are more than 100 children living at the orphanage. Abebech also runs a school there for the orphans and 200 local children.

THE ORPHANAGE
Tadesse has lived at the orphanage since he was five years old. He shares a dormitory with ten other children. He especially likes his bed, which has a light above it so that he can read his books and do his homework. The orphanage provides Tadesse with food, clothes, and everything he needs, and he likes living there very much. The children call the women who look after them "mothers".

This is the logo (symbol) of the Abebech Gobena Orphanage and School.

This is Abebech Gobena, who is the founder of the orphanage. Before the orphanage was built, Abebech looked after the children in a poultry house for six years.

TADESSE'S FAMILY
Tadesse has four sisters. The eldest is 18 years old and works in the countryside. His other sisters are Azeb, Worknesh, and Zenash. They live at the orphanage, too. Tadesse says that the most important person in the world to him is Abebech Gobena. And although Tadesse doesn't have any real brothers, the other boys at the orphanage are like brothers to him.

Tadesse goes to St. John's Church every Sunday.

TADESSE'S CHURCH
Tadesse is a Christian, and this is the church that he goes to on Sundays. Tadesse prays every night, and says that God makes the orphanage a peaceful place. Tadesse believes that at the end of time, all the people who have died will live again. He believes that God will then decide who has been good and who has been bad. The good people will go to Heaven, and the bad people will go to Hell.

Worknesh is 12 years old.

Azeb is 14 years old.

This writing says: "Student Tadesse Assefa is awarded this certificate for his good conduct. This certificate is given to him with many thanks from the Orphanage".

TADESSE'S PRIZE
Tadesse recently won a prize for his school work, and he was presented with this certificate. He learns maths, Amharic (Ethiopia's main language), English, science, social studies, and music. Tadesse likes to learn maths, because he says that if he cannot calculate figures properly, he might be cheated by shopkeepers. He also likes learning English, because he thinks it will help him in the future. Tadesse and the other children also play sport at school.

With the *shorba*, the children eat bread, which is called *dabo*.

Shorba

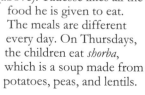

MEALS AT THE ORPHANAGE
Abebech Gobena owns a farm near Addis Ababa. Most of the food that the orphanage needs is grown on this farm. Grain is turned into flour at the orphanage, in a special food processing centre (above). Tadesse likes all the food he is given to eat. The meals are different every day. On Thursdays, the children eat *shorba*, which is a soup made from potatoes, peas, and lentils.

This is Tadesse's youngest sister, Zenash. She is six years old.

Tadesse's name is pronounced *Tad-eh-say*.

"I wear this black thread around my neck because I am a Christian. It shows that I have been baptized."

ታደሰ

"This is how I write my name, Tadesse. When I grow up, I want to do something very important and very good for people, so maybe I will be a medical person, a teacher, or an engineer. If I could wish for anything, it would be that the world was peaceful, so that children could be safe and not frightened. I am scared of war – war destroys everything. It destroys the forest and the animals, and people have no food. Nothing bad has happened to me since I came to the orphanage. I am always happy here."

"I am wearing my favourite track suit. I like to wear warm clothes with long sleeves. It gets very cold in the evenings here, although it is hot in the daytime."

TADESSE'S TOYS AND GAMES
Every morning, when the staff make the children's beds, they put cuddly toys on the covers. This woollen teddy is Tadesse's favourite toy. Tadesse likes playing football with his friends at the orphanage, and watching films and music programmes on television. Tadesse especially likes fast music. He also likes reading stories and books about Ethiopia.

TADESSE'S FRIEND
This is Tadesse with his best friend, Adissu. Adissu is two years older than Tadesse. When Tadesse has difficult homework to do, Adissu helps him with it.

Zenash is wearing her favourite jumper and denim skirt. The orphanage makes or buys all of the children's clothes.

"This is my maths book. The writing on the page is in Amharic, which is the language that I speak and write."

"I like to wear training shoes with my track suit."

45

Asia

Japanese lantern

Indian meal

Korean postbox

ASIA IS THE WORLD'S largest continent. It lies mostly in the northern hemisphere, and stretches from the frozen lands of Siberia in the north, to the tropical rainforests of Indonesia in the south. In between are some of the world's most inhospitable places. The Asian interior experiences baking hot summers and bitterly cold winters.

PEOPLE IN ASIA
More than two-thirds of the world's population lives in Asia. There are more than 40 countries, and a huge variety of cultures and languages. Asians live in all kinds of environments, from the remote mountain kingdoms of the Himalayas to the busy cities of India and China. The children in this section of the book come from China, Mongolia, Japan, South Korea, India, Israel, and Jordan.

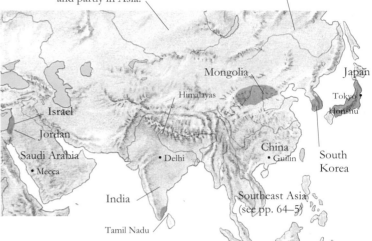

The Russian Federation is the largest country in the world. It is partly in Europe, and partly in Asia.

The cold northern lands of Russia are called Siberia.

Mongolia
Japan
Himalayas
Tokyo
Honshu
Israel
Jordan
China
Guilin
South Korea
Saudi Arabia
Delhi
Mecca
India
Southeast Asia (see pp. 64–5)
Tamil Nadu

Asia is home to the tiger. This magnificent big cat is now an endangered species. Much of its habitat has been destroyed, and many tigers have been poached for their skins.

HOME OF THE SNOWS
The Himalayas are the highest mountains in the world. Their highest peak, Mount Everest (left), soars to 8,848 m (29,028 ft). Himalaya is a Nepalese word. It means "home of the snows".

CHINESE LANDSCAPES
China is the third largest country in the world. Its population numbers more than a billion, which means that one in five people in the world lives in China. China has a huge variety of landscapes, including mountains, deserts, and forests. The town of Guilin in southern China (right) is surrounded by tall limestone hills.

FACES OF ASIA
These children come from all over the Asian continent.

Natsuke, age five, from Japan

Zein, age seven, from Jordan

Shi, age eight, from Israel

Wang Xiang Yi, age nine, from China

Mendbayar, age nine, from Mongolia

Park Jin-Joo, age eleven, from South Korea

46

CHILDREN IN ASIA
These are the Asian children you will be meeting in this section of the book. They come from the Far East, India, and the Middle East.

Guo Shuang is from China (see pp. 48–9).

Daisuke is from Japan (see pp. 52–3).

Meena is from northern India (see pp. 56–7).

Michael is from Israel (see pp. 60–1).

Erdene is from Mongolia (see pp. 50–1).

Yong-Koo and Ji-Koo are from South Korea (see pp. 54–5).

Sarala is from southern India (see pp. 58–9).

Sabah is from Jordan (see pp. 62–3).

SACRED MOUNTAIN
Mount Fuji (left) in Japan is 3,776 m (12,389 ft) high. This famous volcano, which last erupted in 1707, is sacred to the Japanese people. Japan is situated on an unstable part of the Earth's crust, so it often has volcanic eruptions and earthquakes.

BUSY CITIES
Many East Asian cities, such as Beijing (the capital of China) and Seoul (the capital of South Korea), are busy, bustling places, with large populations. Tokyo (left), the capital city of Japan, is home to more than 40 million people. Tokyo's underground railway system becomes so crowded during the rush hour, that the guards have to push and squeeze the commuters into the carriages.

Mongolian hat

Fish, India

TAJ MAHAL
The Taj Mahal (right) is in Agra, northern India. It is a 17th-century mausoleum (a large, magnificent tomb) that was built in white marble by the emperor Shah Jahan, in memory of his wife.

HOLY PLACES
There are many sacred sites in Asia. They include Mecca in Saudi Arabia (right), which is sacred to Muslims. Mecca is the birthplace of the prophet Mohammed. Muslims try to visit Mecca at least once in their lifetime.

Lion statue, Mongolia

Chinese money

V. Harish, age eight, from India

Nerguitsetseg, age ten, from Mongolia

Omar, age seven, from Jordan

T. Swapna, age nine, from India

Yuang Shuai, age eleven, from China

Hana, age seven, from Japan

Sim Ki-Seop, age eleven, from South Korea

Guo Shuang

NINE-YEAR-OLD GUO SHUANG lives with her parents and grandparents just outside Beijing, the capital city of China. Beijing is situated in northeastern China, and its name means "capital of the north". It is a large, busy city, with more than ten million inhabitants. Guo Shuang's parents both work in a local bank. Chinese people put their family name first and their "given" name second. Guo is the family name. In China, people usually address each other using both names, so Shuang is called Guo Shuang.

"This is my favourite toy. I play 'house' with her. My parents gave her to me. She doesn't have a name."

THE GREAT WALL
The Great Wall of China stretches for 2,400 km (1,500 miles), from the Chinese coast to the deserts of central Asia. The Chinese began building the wall about 2,000 years ago, to keep out invaders from the north. It was rebuilt during the 15th century. This section of the wall (above) is about 70 km (45 miles) from Beijing.

Li Xiao Dong, Guo Shuang's mother

Guo Jing Dong, Guo Shuang's father

Sun Pei Lan, Guo Shuang's grandmother

This is Beijing. Tong Xian (pronounced *Tong Shee-en*), where Guo Shuang's family lives is a suburb of Beijing.

Guo Yan, Guo Shuang's grandfather

THE FORBIDDEN CITY
In the centre of Beijing there is an area called the Forbidden City, where Chinese emperors used to live. For hundreds of years, only emperors and their courtiers were allowed there. This temple (left) is just one of the 800 buildings in the Forbidden City.

Guo Shuang's grandparents are wearing traditional Chinese clothes.

Guo Shuang

Trees and flowers grow in the courtyard.

GUO SHUANG'S FAMILY
Guo Shuang calls her parents "Baba" and "Mama". She calls her grandfather "Ye Ye", and her grandmother "Nai Nai". Like most Chinese children, Guo Shuang has no brothers or sisters. More than a billion people live in China, and the government is worried that there will not be enough food and land for everyone if the population grows any bigger. So these days most families have only one child.

GUO SHUANG'S HOME
Guo Shuang's home is built of bricks, with a tiled roof. The house has six rooms, built around an open courtyard. There is a kitchen, a living room, three bedrooms, and a storeroom. The family shares a bathroom with several other families. Guo Shuang's favourite part of the house is the living room, because it has a TV, and a fish tank with 20 goldfish.

"My favourite food is rice. I don't really like meat — boys like meat, and girls prefer fish."

Mantou (steamed bread)

Guo Shuang uses chopsticks to eat her meals.

Guo Shuang's food bowl

Spoon for drinking soup

The dumplings are cooked and ready to eat.

HOME-MADE DUMPLINGS
Sun Pei Lan and a friend are making dumplings in the kitchen (left). They are filling them with meat, onions, garlic, and ginger.

WHAT'S FOR SUPPER?
Guo Shuang usually has meat and vegetables for supper, with rice or steamed bread, called *mantou*.

"In the holidays I wear these ribbons in my hair. But we are not allowed to wear ribbons to school."

"My hair is very long – I can almost sit on it. I usually wear it in plaits, like this. We have to tie our hair up for school."

Guo Shuang's name is pronounced *Gwo Shwang.*

郭 爽

"This is how I write my name, Guo Shuang. Shuang means 'big-hearted, happy, and clean'. When I grow up, I want to be a handicrafts teacher because I love making things. I don't really want to grow up though, because grown-ups don't have as much time to play as children. When I'm not playing, I love reading, especially fairy stories. I like watching cartoons on TV, too."

Guo Shuang wears this cap on her way home from school. The writing on the front says "Safety".

"I wear my coat when the weather is cold. Sometimes it snows here in winter, and then we make snowmen. I love snow."

"Red is my favourite colour for clothes. I am allowed to choose most of my clothes myself."

WE LIKE RED
Guo Shuang and her best friend, Yu Li, are wearing their school uniform, which is a track suit. The children can choose a blue uniform or a red uniform. Guo Shuang and Yu Li prefer to wear red. If the weather is cold, they wear a jumper underneath.

GOING HOME TOGETHER
Guo Shuang starts school at seven o'clock in the morning, and finishes at half past four in the afternoon. She studies maths, Chinese, music, handicrafts, and physical education. The children all walk home together so that they get there safely. They put on their yellow caps and form a long line. The child at the front holds a flag. Then they walk in single file, dropping the children at their homes one by one.

Guo Shuang can write more than 1,000 characters. She hopes to learn about 8,000 by the time she leaves school.

Guo Shuang's school books

Guo Shuang wears this red scarf to show that she belongs to a children's organization called the Young Pioneers.

"Young Pioneers do good deeds in the community, such as helping elderly people."

Guo Shuang usually wears cloth shoes.

"My favourite lesson is handicrafts. I made this mask at school by myself. I cut it out of paper, then I coloured it in."

WRITING CHINESE
Chinese people write using characters rather than letters. There are almost 60,000 characters, but many are hardly ever used. Some represent whole words, and others join together to form words.

This is Guo Shuang's physical education class. Today the children are acting in a play.

49

Erdene

Erdene's family lay a type of rug called a *hivs* on the seats in their home. The decoration on this *hivs* represents an endless knot.

ERDENE IS TEN YEARS OLD and he comes from Mongolia in central Asia. He lives in a remote area called Tsaluu, where his family breeds horses, cows, sheep, and goats. For most of the week Erdene, his parents, and his youngest sister, Oyon Erdene, live in a village 9 km (6 miles) from Tsaluu, so that Erdene and Oyon Erdene can go to school there. They return to Tsaluu at weekends and during the school holidays.

CHILLY HILLS
Tsaluu is surrounded by rolling, grassy hills. There are no trees and hardly any people there – Mongolia has one of the smallest populations for its size in the world. Tsaluu is cold almost all year round. In winter the temperature can drop to -50°C (-58°F).

Erdene calls his father and mother "Aav" and "Eej".

Rentsen, Erdene's father

Narangarav, Erdene's niece

Batmunkh's name means "strong forever".

Buddha statue in a Mongolian temple

"When I feel scared at night, I hold my Buddha amulet [charm]. Then I feel safe again."

PRAYING AT HOME
Erdene's family are Buddhists. They usually pray at home, because the nearest temple is many kilometres away.

Erdene | Oyon Erdene | Badamsuren, Erdene's mother | Tserenpagma, Batmunkh's wife | Erdene Garav, Tserenpagma's niece

ERDENE'S FAMILY
Erdene's father, Rentsen, spends most of the day looking after the animals. His mother, Badamsuren, is an accountant in Sergelen, where Erdene goes to school. After work she does the household chores and milks the cows. Erdene has two grown-up brothers, called Batmunkh and Munkhbat, and an older sister, called Ulziihuu. Batmunkh is married and has a one-year-old daughter.

During the week, Erdene lives in this house in Sergelen.

LIVING IN GERS
Erdene's home in Tsaluu is a large, circular tent called a *ger*. *Gers* were developed hundreds of years ago to suit the nomadic way of life followed by most Mongolian people. They are easy to take down and transport from place to place. Although many Mongolians are no longer nomadic, *gers* are still the most popular type of home.

The white canvas that covers the *ger* is held in place with ropes made from horses' tails.

The *ger's* wooden frame is covered with a thick layer of felt to keep out the cold.

There is a hole in the *ger's* roof for the chimney, and to let in the light.

There is a stove in the centre of the *ger* for heating and cooking. The family uses dried cow dung for fuel.

Erdene's cousin Erdene Garav is four years old. She lives with Erdene's family in Tsaluu.

Erdene's pointed hat is called a *janjin malgai*.

"When I grow up, I want to learn how to drive a car. I like being a child, though, because I can enter the children's horse races."

Erdene uses this herding stick for rounding up the animals.

Erdene's name is pronounced *Ehr-den-nay*.

Эрдэнэсүрэн

"This is how I write my name, Erdene. It means 'something precious'. My full name is Rentsen Erdene – Rentsen is my father's name. My favourite time of year is summer, because it is warm and I can ride my horse and help with the herding. Once when I was out herding, a wolf appeared. I was very scared, and I ran away. The most exciting thing in the world is horse-racing. Every July I take part in races. About 300 riders enter – I don't often win."

FUN WITH BONES
Erdene plays a horse-racing game with these pieces, which are called *shagai*.

Shagai pieces are made from sheeps' ankle bones.

These bones are dyed different colours with tree sap.

ERDENE'S FRIEND
Erdene's best friend is called Amraa. They like to play table tennis together, and they often wrestle with each other.

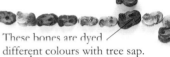

Erdene's cloth belt is called a *bus*.

"We have a television, but I prefer to be outside, riding my horse or herding the animals. I also love to sing Mongolian songs."

Erdene's school

ERDENE'S LESSONS
Erdene's favourite lesson is physical education, because he loves running around. He also learns maths, literature, and the Mongolian language. Modern Mongolian is written using the Cyrillic alphabet, but the traditional Mongolian script is now being taught again. Erdene is learning how to write using both scripts.

This is Erdene's Cyrillic writing lesson. The Cyrillic alphabet was introduced into Mongolia by the Russians in the 1940s.

"We have two dogs, called Banhar and Hoilog. This one is Hoilog."

When Erdene is riding, he cracks his whip in the air to make his horse gallop faster.

ALL SORTS OF ANIMALS
Erdene's family has 30 horses, 9 cows, and about 120 sheep and goats. Erdene has his own horse (above right), which he rides every day during the summer.

Erdene's mother made this traditional Mongolian coat, which is called a *deel*. It is made of cotton and lined with soft lambswool. The *deel* keeps Erdene warm throughout the cold winter months.

These Mongolian boots with upturned toes are called *Mongol gutal*.

MONGOLIAN MEALS
It is difficult to grow crops in Mongolia's harsh climate, but the land is ideal for grazing sheep. So Mongolians eat a lot of mutton (sheep) and not many vegetables. One of Erdene's favourite meals is mutton noodle soup, which is called *guriltai shol*.

Guriltai shol

These biscuits, called *boortsog*, are made from flour and water boiled in oil.

Daisuke

DAISUKE TASHITA IS TEN years old and lives near the town of Ogawa in Japan. Daisuke's family runs an organic farm, growing crops and raising animals in ways that do not harm the environment. For example, Daisuke's parents never use chemical fertilizers or pesticides on their crops. The family even produces its own electricity, using the gas given off by animal manure, called biogas, to power a generator.

TOKYO
Ogawa is not far from Tokyo (above), which is Japan's busy capital city. Daisuke often goes there with his parents. He loves to look around the department stores and bookshops.

Ryuichi, Daisuke's father

Mieko, Daisuke's mother

Daisuke calls his mother "Okahsan" and his father "Otohsan".

Daisuke's little brother, Shota, is four years old.

DAISUKE'S FAMILY
Daisuke's parents work together on the farm, looking after the animals and tending the crops. Daisuke's mother also delivers produce from the farm to people in the town. Daisuke helps his mother with the housework. He lights the fire every day, and washes the dishes after meals.

On the annual Children's Day festival, Japanese families with young boys hang carp-shaped kites outside their homes.

BUNK BEDS AND FUTONS
Like most houses in Japan, Daisuke's home is built of wood. Daisuke shares a bedroom with his brother, Shota, and his sister, Akane. Daisuke and Shota sleep on bunk beds, and Akane sleeps on the floor on a traditional Japanese mattress called a futon. Daisuke would like to sleep on a futon, too, but there is no more room on the floor.

VEGETABLE VARIETIES
Daisuke's farm is surrounded by cultivated fields. His family grows several types of vegetable, including cabbages, radishes, and a type of onion called a Japanese onion. They also grow rice, in a field that they share with four other families. Rice is Japan's most widely grown crop.

"We have three dogs. This one is my favourite. His name is Muku-Muku, which means 'Fluffy'."

Each morning before school, Daisuke collects eggs from the chicken hutches.

CHICKENS GALORE
Daisuke's family keeps about 500 hens. Every day they collect the hens' eggs to sell. There are also ten pigs and two sheep on the farm. The pigs are reared for pork, and the sheep are kept for their wool.

"Akane is seven years old. She always leaves our bedroom in a mess, and I have to clear it up."

"We don't have a school uniform, but we have to wear a yellow cap like this one."

Daisuke is carrying a traditional Japanese school satchel. In Japan, children's satchels have to last them throughout their years at school.

Daisuke's name is pronounced *Die-soo-key.*

田下 大輔

"This is how I write my name. I was very tiny when I was born, and my parents wished that I would grow up to be big and healthy. So they called me Daisuke – *Dai* means 'big'. When I grow up, I want to be a scientist and study dinosaur fossils. I love dinosaurs. Not long ago my grandmother took me to see the dinosaur exhibition at the Tokyo National Museum. It was the most exciting thing that I have ever done. I would love to visit the dinosaur museums in the United States. I have read all about them in my dinosaur books."

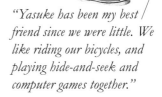

"Yasuke has been my best friend since we were little. We like riding our bicycles, and playing hide-and-seek and computer games together."

"It gets cold here in winter. I like this sweatshirt because it is padded and keeps me warm."

Instead of using ticks, teachers in Japan mark correct school work with these red whirls.

Daisuke's school is called Yawata Primary School.

This is Daisuke's science book. He has been learning about what happens at a fire station.

SCHOOLTIME AND PLAYTIME
Daisuke goes to school six days a week, with one Saturday off each month. His favourite subject is science, and his least favourite subject is maths. At playtime the children usually play a game called "dodgeball". In this game they try to dodge out of the way when the ball is thrown at them.

"Track suit bottoms are my favourite sort of trousers."

Daisuke's dinosaur magazines

"I'd love to ride a dinosaur!"

Daisuke's favourite video game

MAD ABOUT DINOSAURS
Daisuke loves reading books and magazines about dinosaurs, and he enjoys watching dinosaur films on television and at the cinema. He also likes playing video and computer games.

SOMETHING FISHY
Like most Japanese people, Daisuke and his family often eat seafood, such as *sashimi* (raw fish) and seaweed. They also eat vegetables and rice from the farm. Daisuke's favourite meals are pork spare ribs, and *soba* noodles.

Like all Japanese people, Daisuke takes off his shoes before he enters his house. He sometimes wears slippers indoors, but he prefers to go barefoot. Daisuke usually wears sneakers outside the house.

Daisuke's hot water bottle keeps him warm on cold winter nights. It is made of metal, and it gets very hot, so Daisuke wraps it up in a piece of cloth before he puts it in his bed.

Mochi rice cakes with seaweed wrapped around them

Daisuke's chopsticks

Yong-Koo and Ji-Koo

TWIN BROTHERS KANG YONG-KOO and Kang Ji-Koo live in Seoul, the capital city of South Korea in East Asia. They are 11 years old, and Yong-Koo is 10 minutes older than Ji-Koo. The twins live in a flat with their parents, their grandmother, and their sister. The twins' father, Kang Chu-Cheol, runs a glass-cutting factory. Their mother, Kim Min-Sook, looks after the home and makes leather lipstick cases to sell.

Yong-Koo   Ji-Koo

SEOUL
This is the part of the city where Yong-Koo and Ji-Koo live. Seoul is one of the largest cities in the world, with a population of more than 10 million. Much of the city is modern, with high-rise flats and offices, and wide, traffic-filled roads. But between the concrete buildings there are narrow alleyways with ancient royal palaces and beautiful traditional houses.

Lee Soon-Ye, the twins' grandmother

Kang Mi-Wha

Kim Min-Sook

Kang Chu-Cheol

The twins' parents and grandmother are wearing their brightly coloured traditional Korean costume.

YONG-KOO AND JI-KOO'S FAMILY
The twins call their mother and father "Omma" and "Aboji", and their grandmother "Halmoni". Their sister, Kang Mi-Wha, is 13 years old. Yong-Koo gets on well with Mi-Wha, but Ji-Koo often argues with her.

GAZING AT STARS
Yong-Koo and Ji-Koo's home is on the second floor of a block of flats. The twins share one bedroom, and their sister sleeps in another with their grandmother. Yong-Koo and Ji-Koo sleep on mattresses which are stored in their parents' bedroom during the day. The twins' favourite part of their home is the balcony outside the kitchen. They love to go there at night and look at the stars together.

This is how Yong-Koo writes his name.

강 용 구

"Yong means 'brave', and Koo means 'to save'. If I could wish for anything, I would wish that there was no crime. I want to be a lawyer or a judge when I grow up, because then I could make sure that justice is done. I would like to marry a polite and sincere woman. I'd also love to go to Australia, to see the kangaroos and koalas. There are still lots of unspoiled places in Australia."

"Park Chang-Yong is my best friend, because he feels the same way about things as I do."

A LONG DAY AT SCHOOL
Yong-Koo loves doing science experiments and maths at school. Ji-Koo likes the days when they have tests, because the children are allowed to leave early then. The twins usually do other activities after school, including piano lessons and art classes. Sometimes they don't get home from school until nine o'clock at night.

These shoes are for wearing indoors at school.

This is Yong-Koo's natural science and geography book. At the moment the twins are learning about the natural resources of South Korea.

The twins' school is called Shinnam Primary School.

Yong-Koo's maths book

The twins have two pairs of shoes each for school – a pair of indoor shoes and a pair of outdoor shoes. When they are indoors, they keep their outdoor shoes in their school bags.

These robots are Yong-Koo's favourite toys. He loves to take them apart and put them back together again.

SWEET AND SOUR FAVOURITE
The twins' family often eats seafood stews, steamed rice, pork, and spicy cabbage. Yong-Koo's favourite meal is sweet and sour pork, called *tang su yuk*. He says that there is no type of food that he doesn't like.

Tang su yuk

Steamed rice

Yong-Koo's spoon

Chopsticks

Yong-Koo's name is pronounced *Yong-koo*.

"I like autumn, because the leaves turn such beautiful colours."

Ji-Koo's name is pronounced *Chee-koo*.

"I like summer, because it's the holidays and I can play with my friends."

강 지구

"The first part of my name, Ji, means 'wisdom'. I would love to travel into Space, because I want to see if there are any creatures on the other planets. I am also curious about black holes. When I grow up, I want to be a politician so that I can develop my country. I would like to marry a bubbly woman, and have two children, a boy and a girl. I am always wondering how children in other countries live. I would like to ask them, 'Are you well, and are you happy with your life?'"

"Our family is Buddhist. On Sundays we go to the temple. We have Buddhism classes there, and we learn Buddhist songs."

Ji-Koo's best friend is called Shin Dong-Chul. They like to play a ball game called *jae gi* in the school playground.

JI-KOO'S ASSEMBLY BOX
Ji-Koo enjoys making things, like this helicopter, from the pieces in his "assembly box". The box contains lots of plastic parts, nuts, and bolts.

The twins' colourful jackets and trousers are made of silk:

JI-KOO'S FOOD FAVOURITES
Ji-Koo's favourite meals are *kimchi*, and soya bean and vegetable soup, called *twenjang chi-gay*. Kimchi is the most popular dish in Korea. The ingredients of this hot and spicy dish vary, but it is often made from Chinese cabbage, garlic, ginger, and chilli.

Kimchi

Twenjang chi-gay

The twins are wearing their traditional Korean costume, called *hanbok*. Han means "Korean" and *bok* means "clothing". The family wears *hanbok* on special occasions.

The twins usually wear running shoes outside the home.

"The good thing about being a child is that there are lots of possibilities for the future. Grown-ups have already chosen their futures – there are no more possibilities for them."

During school playtime, the children play *jae gi* with this pink tinsel ball.

Meena

MEENA IS SEVEN YEARS OLD and lives in New Delhi, the capital city of India. She was born in the state of Rajasthan, to the west of New Delhi, in a village called Masalpur. This region is very dry, and Meena and her family had to leave their village because there wasn't enough rain for their crops to grow. They now live and work on a construction site in the city, where a factory is being built.

RAJASTHAN
Meena's family comes from the state of Rajasthan in northwest India. This huge state has a variety of landscapes. In the west is the Thar desert, which stretches into neighbouring Pakistan. Further south are areas of forest (above) where tigers stalk their prey, and wild peacocks sit in the trees or peck about on the ground for food.

Meena's mother, Prembai, is wearing a *lehnga* (skirt), a *choli* (blouse), and an *odhni* (long scarf).

Rewal

Suman

Meena

Lachi, Meena's father

Sonu

DELHI
The city of Delhi has two main parts, called New Delhi and Old Delhi. Many of Old Delhi's buildings are built in the Mogul style of architecture. The Moguls were emperors who ruled India from 1526 to 1858. Mogul-style buildings, such as this mosque, often have onion-shaped domes and delicately arched windows and doorways. New Delhi was built by the British, who ruled India from 1858 to 1947.

MEENA'S FAMILY
Both of Meena's parents work on the building site where they live. Meena's father lays bricks, and her mother is a labourer. Meena has two younger brothers, called Rewal and Sonu, and an older sister, called Suman. The family speaks Rajasthani, the language of their state.

Suman looks after her brothers and sister while Prembai and Lachi are working.

Meena's mother reinforces the walls of the house with cow dung.

MEENA'S HOME
Meena's house is built of bricks, with a corrugated iron roof. There is no electricity or water, and no toilet inside the house. When all the work on the construction site is finished, the house will be pulled down. Meena's family will move to the next site, and will build another house to live in.

Shiva is one of the most important gods in Hinduism. He symbolizes the destruction of evil and the continuity of the universe.

MEENA'S RELIGION
Like most people in India, Meena and her family are Hindus. They often visit this shrine (far left), which is close to where they live. Although Hindus believe in one main God, they worship several different gods and goddesses who symbolize different qualities, such as wisdom, purity, and strength.

"My hair is short now. It used to be long, but Papa cut it off."

"This is how I write my name, Meena. It means 'fish'. My dream is to go back to my village. I liked living there because our house was built of stone. I don't like the building site because there are no trees and it is dirty. In our village you can pick berries from the trees, but here in the city you have to pay for them. My favourite animals are cats. I don't like dogs, because they might eat me up. When I grow up, I want to be a labourer, like Ma."

Rukmini   Gaura   Meena   Rajni

MEENA'S FRIENDS
These are some of Meena's friends from the construction site. Rukmini and Rajni are her best friends.

"I like to wear dresses with frills. When I am cold, I put on a jumper."

"Indian girls like to wear bracelets. I feel sad, because I can't get any bracelets to fit me here."

THE CRÈCHE
The children who live on the construction site go to the crèche while their parents are working. Here an adult looks after the younger children while the older children, including Meena, have their lessons. Meena learns Hindi (India's main language) and maths.

"I have written one to ten on my slate. I use these stones to help me count."

Meena's favourite vegetable dish

MEENA'S MEALS
Meena's favourite meal is *chana* (chick-peas), *alu* (potato), and *gobhi* (cauliflower), with *roti* (Indian bread made from wheat flour). Meena's mother cooks the family's meals over a fire, using dried cow dung for fuel.

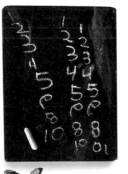

Roti and vegetables

HAIR OIL AND HENNA
Prembai puts hair oil in Meena's hair to make it thick and shiny. She also colours Meena's fingernails with natural dye from the henna plant.

"I usually wear flip-flops on my feet, but today I am cross because a boy has taken them."

Sabah

"This is my sister Iman. She is four years old."

SABAH KHLEIFAT IS NINE YEARS old and lives in Jordan. She belongs to the Bedouin people, who live in the desert regions of North Africa and the Middle East. The Bedouin are nomads, which means that they move from place to place in search of fresh vegetation for their animals. Many Bedouin, including Sabah's family, are now settling down in towns and villages. But during the hot summer months, Sabah's family moves into a traditional Bedouin tent.

DESERT DWELLERS
The name Bedouin is Arabic for "desert dwellers". Sabah's village is called Taybeh. It is surrounded by rugged, barren hills, with steep-sided desert valleys, called wadis. This part of Jordan only has a small amount of rain. The wadis are usually dry, and there is little vegetation on the hillsides.

Sabah's father, Abdul, winds a length of cloth around his head to make a *hatta*.

Deebeh, Sabah's mother

Abdul's warm woollen coat is called a *farwa*. He only needs to wear it during the cold winter months.

These sturdy boots are ideal for life in the desert.

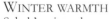
Deebeh always wears a long dress.

SABAH'S FAMILY
There are 28 people in Sabah's family. They are Sabah, her father, her father's two wives, her grandmother, her 11 brothers and sisters, and her 12 half-brothers and half-sisters. The youngest of Sabah's brothers and sisters is 14 months old, and the oldest is 24 years old. Sabah's father, Abdul, is a carpenter. He also looks after the family's sheep, which they keep for their milk and meat. Sabah calls her father "Ya-ba" and her mother "Ya-ma".

Here are 10 of Sabah's 23 brothers and sisters.

Khitam

Mohammed and Ibrahim

Yusef and Usama   Zenab Sabah Badriah   Hind   Iman and Saed

WINTER WARMTH
Sabah's winter home consists of two stone houses. One house is for the men, and the other is for the women. Sabah's favourite part of her home is the salon, where the family entertains guests. This large room has cushions around the walls for sitting on. Bedouins are very hospitable people. It is part of their tradition that no stranger should ever be turned away.

When the cold winter weather arrives, Sabah and her family move into their winter home.

SUMMER COOL
During the summer, when daytime temperatures can soar to more than 40°C (104°F), Sabah's family lives in a large tent (left). The floor of the tent is covered with rugs and cushions, and there are mattresses for sleeping on. To keep the tent cool, the family props open the sides so that breezes can blow through. Bedouin tents are usually made from goat hair. Their Arabic name, *bayt ash-sha'ar*, means "house of hair".

"I made these two teapots in my craft lesson at school. They are made of clay."

"This is my brother Saed. He is seven years old."

Sabah's name is pronounced *Sa-ba.*

"This is how I write my name, Sabah. It means 'morning'. The land around my village is very beautiful. My favourite time of year here is spring, because then the hills are green and there are lots of flowers. I don't like the summer, because there is no rain and the flowers wither and die. And winter is too cold – sometimes it snows. When I grow up, I want to be a teacher. I would like to teach children who are about six years old. If I could wish for anything, it would be for all the children of the world to be happy."

PLAYING "GUESTS"

Sabah likes to play with her half-sisters Zenab, Hind, and Badria. Their favourite game is called "guests". The sisters pretend to be grown-ups entertaining people in their homes. They take it in turns to be the host.

"I like to wear all sorts of clothes, but dresses are my favourites. In winter I put on lots of layers to keep warm. Today the weather is cold, and I am wearing jeans and a jumper underneath my dress."

Sabah's school

NO WORRIES

Sabah's school day begins at seven o'clock in the morning and finishes at 12 noon. Sabah loves all her lessons, and says there is nothing at school for her to worry about. Sabah's favourite lesson is maths. She also learns Arabic and social studies.

"I wish I had some gold necklaces to wear with my dress."

This is Sabah's Arabic writing book. Arabic is Jordan's main language.

"These are my school books. In my maths book you can see that I am learning all about measurement, and how to draw a square. I have written 'The End' several times at the back of my Arabic writing book."

Sabah's maths book

MEALTIME MAYHEM

Sabah's family often has *shurba*, which is a type of soup made from yogurt, rice, onions, and pasta. With the soup they eat a type of flat bread, called *khobz*. The family eat their meals together in the salon. There are so many children that sometimes their parents don't notice that some of them are still playing outside. By the time they come in, everything has been eaten up!

Khobz

Shurba

Tuk-tuk, Thailand

Limes, Thailand

Vietnamese money

Southeast Asia and Australasia

IN THE SOUTHEASTERN CORNER of Asia lie the countries of Burma, Thailand, Laos, Cambodia, Vietnam, Malaysia, and Singapore. A long chain of islands continues southeast towards Australia, forming the Philippines and Indonesia. The continent of Australasia consists of Australia, New Zealand, and several neighbouring South Pacific islands.

PEOPLE OF SOUTHEAST ASIA AND AUSTRALASIA
This region is home to many ethnic groups, including the hill tribes of Thailand and Vietnam, the rainforest tribes of Indonesia, and the Aboriginal Australians. Many Southeast Asian people live in farming and fishing villages, while others live in modern cities such as Singapore. The children in this section of the book come from Vietnam, Thailand, the Philippines, Indonesia, New Zealand, and Australia.

ASIA
Vietnam
Thailand
Philippines
Malaysia
Panay
Singapore
Sulawesi
Indonesia
Bali
Western Australia
AUSTRALASIA
North Island
New Zealand

TROPICAL FORESTS
Lush forests, such as this rainforest in Malaysia (left), thrive in Southeast Asia's hot, wet climate.

SINGAPORE
The modern city of Singapore sits at the tip of the Malaysian peninsula, on the shipping routes between the Indian and Pacific Oceans. About 25,000 ships dock at Singapore's busy port every year.

EMPTY ISLANDS
Bali (right) is one of the 13,677 islands which make up Indonesia. More than half of the Indonesian islands are uninhabited.

FACES OF SOUTHEAST ASIA AND AUSTRALASIA
These children come from all over the region.

Michiko and Makoto, age ten and six, from Australia

Karika, age eleven, from New Zealand

Ta Ta, age eight, from the Philippines

Pham Dieu Trang, age eight, from Vietnam

Yaso, age seven, from Indonesia

Jessica, age eight, from Australia

Emung, age nine, from Thailand

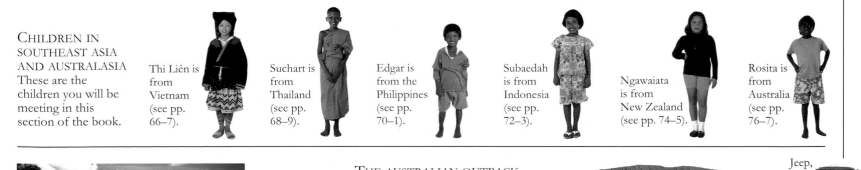

CHILDREN IN SOUTHEAST ASIA AND AUSTRALASIA

These are the children you will be meeting in this section of the book.

Thi Liên is from Vietnam (see pp. 66–7).

Suchart is from Thailand (see pp. 68–9).

Edgar is from the Philippines (see pp. 70–1).

Subaedah is from Indonesia (see pp. 72–3).

Ngawaiata is from New Zealand (see pp. 74–5).

Rosita is from Australia (see pp. 76–7).

RICE TERRACES
Rice is Southeast Asia's main crop, and it is grown all over the region. In mountainous areas, terraces are cut into the hillsides (above). These terraces trap rainwater which is needed to flood the rice fields. They also prevent the soil from being swept away down the mountainsides.

TALES FROM THE TEMPLE
At temple festivals in Bali, dancers dress in elaborate costumes. Many Balinese dances tell religious legends, such as the ancient Hindu epic, called the *Ramayana*.

THE AUSTRALIAN OUTBACK
Australia's vast interior is called the Outback. Much of the Outback consists of flat, red-coloured desert dotted with ancient rocky outcrops, such as Uluru, or Ayers Rock (right). Uluru is an Aboriginal name meaning "Great Pebble".

Jeep, Philippines

PARADISE ISLANDS
The Pacific Ocean covers two-thirds of the Earth's surface. Many islands are scattered across this vast expanse of water. Some, such as Tahiti (left), are volcanic. Others, called atolls, are made of coral (the skeletons of tiny marine animals). Coral grows in the shallow waters of warm, tropical seas. In this aerial photograph you can see the coral reefs that fringe Tahiti.

Vietnamese spices

NEW ZEALAND
New Zealand is made up of two islands, called North Island and South Island. The southwest coast of South Island is deeply indented with fjords, such as Milford Sound (right). These fjords were scoured out by glaciers during the last Ice Age. New Zealand's dramatic scenery attracts visitors from all over the world.

Australian postbox

Lotus flowers, Thailand

Byron, age eleven, from New Zealand

Chinda, age twelve, from Thailand

Aisha, age nine, from the Philippines

Carly, age nine (and Zip the rabbit), from Australia

Hernah, age ten, from Indonesia

Nguyen Hoang Anh, age ten, from Vietnam

Vu Dieu Thao, age nine, from Vietnam

Thi Liên

THI LIÊN IS NINE YEARS old and lives in the mountains of northern Vietnam. She belongs to a tribe of hill people called the Dao. Thi Liên's family lives in a tiny community called Tam, which is 4 km (2.5 miles) from the nearest village. They are self-sufficient, growing their own food and making many of their own clothes. The community has its own supply of hydro-electricity, which is powered by water from a nearby lake.

Lotus flowers

"Liên means 'lotus flower'."

A HOME IN THE HILLS
Thi Liên's home is built of wood, with a tiled roof and a floor of earth. The porch in front is shaded by a thatched roof. Thi Liên sleeps in a bed with her mother, and her brothers share another bed with their father. Thi Liên likes to sit at her school desk, which she is allowed to take home during the school holidays.

BEAUTIFUL BATIK
Ban Thi Son uses a technique called batik to make patterns on pieces of cloth. She puts wax on the parts that she wants to leave white, then she dyes the cloth. When it has changed colour, she removes the wax, leaving the white patterns underneath.

Thi Liên's father is called Van Hoan, which means "perfect".

Thi Liên's mother, Ban Thi Son, likes to chew betel-nuts. These nuts stain her teeth black.

Thi Liên's mother uses a plant called indigo to dye cloth dark blue.

"This is my brother Van Minh. Boys have 'Van' in their name, and girls have 'Thi' in theirs."

Batik tools

Lid

Ban Thi Son keeps her tools in this bamboo tube.

Wax

Thi Liên   Van Thang

THI LIÊN'S FAMILY
Thi Liên's parents are farmers. They grow rice, corn, cassava, and fruit trees. Thi Liên's mother also looks after the home and makes clothes for the family. Thi Liên calls her "Mé". Thi Liên has two brothers. Van Minh is twelve years old, and Van Thang is seven years old.

This rice has been husked and is ready to be cooked.

Wooden machine for husking rice

The local children love to ride on the buffalos' backs.

ANIMALS ALL AROUND
In the hill-tribe villages, people keep chickens and pigs for food, and water buffalos to pull the ploughs in the fields. Thi Liên's family also has a pet dog called Lu. Thi Liên's favourite animal is a piglet that belongs to one of her neighbours.

FEEDING TIME
Thi Liên feeds the chickens, which live in this wooden shed (right). They eat corn and leftover food scraps. She also looks after the pig, which eats sweet potatoes and banana plants. Van Thang and Van Minh help their father to look after the family's buffalo.

HUSKING THE RICE
After picking the rice, Thi Liên's mother has to husk it (take it out of its dry outer covering) before it can be cooked and eaten. She uses this wooden machine (left) for husking the rice.

"My hair is brown, but you can't see it because it's covered with this scarf. Mé helps me to dress and put on my headscarf."

"I am wearing my traditional Dao outfit, called a lamchu. *It has several different pieces. There is a scarf, a skirt, a jacket, and the* hang pen, *which I wrap around my legs."*

Bamboo sheath for carrying the knife

Thi Liên's necklace was made by one of the people in the village, using old kitchen utensils. First the metal was beaten flat, then it was bent into this round shape.

Thi Liên's name is pronounced *Tee Lee-an.* The name of her tribe, the Dao, is pronounced *Zow.*

Thi Liên's knife for chopping wood

Thi Liên's basket for carrying firewood

Thi Liên's mother made this *lamchu*. It took her about a year. First she made the batik cloth, then she added the embroidery using thread dyed with natural colours from plants.

"I wear my lamchu *to school and when I visit the village. I don't like to get it dirty, so I wear other clothes to play in. But I like wearing the* lamchu *best of all."*

Thi Liên

"My name is Trieu Thi Liên. We say our family name first, then our 'given' name. When I grow up, I want to be an agricultural engineer and develop new ways of growing rice. Rice farming is difficult here in the mountains, because people have to carry heavy baskets up steep slopes. I think it must be much easier down on the plains. It would be very useful to learn about science and technology."

A GAME WITH STICKS
Thi Liên uses these sticks and a small piece of fruit to play her favourite game, *truyen.* She lays one stick down, then puts the others across it, like this. Then she throws the fruit in the air and picks up one stick before catching it again. She carries on until she is holding all the sticks in one hand. Then she plays again, picking up two sticks at a time, then three, then four, until finally she picks them all up in one go.

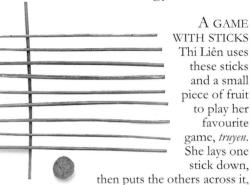

Thi Liên's school

Every day Thi Liên collects firewood for her mother. She splits the wood in two with her special knife, and carries it home in this basket.

SCHOOL IN THE MORNING
Thi Liên starts school at eight o'clock in the morning, and finishes three hours later. She likes literature and maths, and thinks that they are easy. Thi Liên speaks her tribal language, Dao, at home, and the national language, Vietnamese, at school.

Thi Liên has been doing her maths in this exercise book. The writing is in Vietnamese.

A squeeze of lime adds extra flavour to Thi Liên's meals.

FOOD FROM THE HILLS
Thi Liên's family often eats rice noodles, which they call *pho.* With the *pho* they eat vegetables, and sometimes chicken or pork. Thi Liên's favourite food is fruit. Her family grows limes, bananas, plums, apricots, bananas, guavas, and jack fruit.

Chicken and vegetables

Chilli sauce

Thi Liên eats her food with wooden chopsticks.

Suchart

SUCHART BAISI LIVES in a temple called Wat Tanot in the city of Ayuthaya in Thailand. Suchart is 12 years old, and he is studying to become a Buddhist monk. Traditionally, young men in Thailand spend some time as novices, even if only for a few weeks. But Suchart would like to be a monk for the rest of his life. Suchart's mother is dead. His father, who is a pineapple farmer, lives with Suchart's two sisters further south in Thailand.

WAT TANOT
Fourteen monks and 34 novices live at Wat Tanot. *Wat* is the Thai word for temple, and *tanot* means sugar palm, a type of tree that grows nearby. Suchart meditates on the teachings of Buddha in the temple for half an hour every day.

Phra Maha Surachai is the abbot (head of the temple).

Suchart

The novices' robes are made of cotton.

Inside the temple grounds, the novices leave their right shoulders bare. They cover them up when they perform religious functions or go outside the temple.

The robes are held in place with a sash.

AROUND THE TEMPLE
The temple buildings at Wat Tanot overlook a beautiful fish pond. The monks keep carp in the pond, and Suchart enjoys feeding these fish. There are many temples in Ayuthaya, which was Thailand's capital city between A.D. 1350 and 1767. During this time, 33 different kings ruled the country.

The monks take off their sandals when they enter the temple.

THE MONKS' ROBES
Thai Buddhist monks wear flowing, saffron-coloured robes. The robes are made of two pieces of cloth, worn with a sash around the waist.

Suchart sits cross-legged on his bed when he meditates.

SUCHART'S HUT
Each of the monks and novices at the temple has his own hut to sleep in. Suchart's hut has a roof made of palm leaves and a floor made of bamboo. Thailand is a hot country, and Suchart keeps his hut cool by propping open the door with bamboo sticks.

ANIMALS AT THE TEMPLE
More than 20 cats live at Wat Tanot. They are strays that have been brought to the temple by the local people, who know that they will be well cared for there. Suchart likes cats, but his favourite animals are dogs. He is afraid of snakes, because they are poisonous and might bite him.

INSIDE THE HUT
Suchart likes his hut because it is a quiet, peaceful place. There is an electric light bulb, so he can read his books after dark. Around the walls are shelves where he keeps his things. Suchart sleeps on a thin mat, with a pillow, a blanket, and a mosquito net to stop insects from biting him in the night.

"The naughtiest thing I ever did was to climb on to the roof at home to pick papaya fruit."

The novices have their heads and eyebrows shaved once a month. Their hair must not grow more than an inch long.

"I don't wear any jewellery. Many Thai people wear a Buddha amulet [charm], but I don't need one because Buddha is inside me, protecting me."

Suchart's name is pronounced *Soo-chart*.

"I don't have any toys, but I love to play football with the other novices. There is a television here that we can watch once a week, but I don't really like television."

"I keep my personal belongings inside this satchel. It was given to me by the monks in my home town of Ratchaburi."

"This is my name, Suchart, written in Thai script. It means 'One who is born into a good life'. The other novices here call me 'Noy', which means 'small'. I was born in the year 2524 B.E. (Buddhist Era), which means 2,524 years since the Lord Buddha died. I was brought to Ayuthaya by my teacher from home, because I can continue with my Buddhist studies here. I want to be a monk when I grow up, because it is a simple life. I don't want to be an abbot, because that would be more complicated. I don't really wish for anything at all. I am happy here just as I am."

BUDDHIST STUDIES

There are two sets of classes a day at the temple, and the novices take it in turns to study, either in the mornings or in the afternoons. The novices study two subjects: Buddhism and Pali. Pali is the ancient language in which all of Buddha's teachings were written.

Suchart is learning how to write Pali words. He likes studying Pali, because he will soon be able to learn to translate Buddha's teaching.

"This morning the villagers put rice, lotus flowers, joss sticks, and a candle in my alms bowl."

Rice

Lotus flowers

Joss (incense) sticks

Candle

EARLY MEALS

The novices get up at about five o'clock in the morning. Before breakfast they walk around the local village with their alms bowls. The villagers put offerings for the temple, such as food and flowers, into the bowls. Suchart eats breakfast at about seven o'clock, and lunch at eleven o'clock. Buddhist monks are not supposed to eat after midday, so lunch is Suchart's last meal of the day.

"I don't like wearing sandals because I am always losing them. We have to take off our sandals all the time, whenever we eat and pray, and I always forget where I have put them."

Fish curry

Rice

String beans

Chilli in fish sauce is added to meals to make them spicy.

Edgar

EDGAR FLORES IS EIGHT YEARS OLD and lives in the Philippines, a group of more than 7,000 islands in Southeast Asia. Edgar's family lives by the sea on the island of Panay, in a village called Villa Rica de Arevalo. His father buys oysters from a local oyster farmer, opens them, and sells them to restaurants. Edgar and his older brother open oysters too, before and after school.

This is Edgar's little brother Edwin.

PHILIPPINE FIELDS
The Philippine islands have a hot season, a cool season, and a rainy season. The climate is ideal for growing rice, and there are rice fields (above) all along the coast of Panay. Inland, there are high mountains. People grow rice on the steep slopes by cutting flat terraces into the hillsides. Some of the rice terraces are more than 2,000 years old.

Eduardo, Edgar's father

Mariluz, Edgar's mother

Weng Weng

Bap Bap

Edwin

Edgar

BAMBOO HOME
Edgar's home is made from bamboo, which grows around the village. The walls are loosely woven, so that the wind can pass through them and keep the house cool. There are two rooms in the house. The bedroom is divided into two halves. Edgar's parents sleep in one half, and the children sleep in the other half. During the rainy season, rain sometimes drips through the roof. The children find a dry corner and cover themselves with blankets to keep warm. Edgar's favourite part of the house is the window ledge. He sits there to open oysters.

EDGAR'S FAMILY
Edgar calls his parents "Papang" and "Mamang". He has three brothers. They are Bap Bap, who is twelve years old, Edwin, who is three years old, and baby Weng Weng. When Edgar's parents go out, Edgar looks after Edwin and Weng Weng. He also helps his mother in the kitchen, and collects water from the pump nearby for drinking and washing.

GOING TO CHURCH
Like most Filipino families, Edgar's family follows the Catholic religion. The church in Edgar's village shares a priest with another church, and Edgar's family goes to church whenever the priest holds a service. Edgar says that when he dies, his body will go into the ground and his soul will go to Heaven.

FISHING FOR FRY
As well as opening oysters, Edgar and Bap Bap catch tiny young fish, called fry. They trap the fry in shallow waters, using a net tied to wooden poles. Bap Bap sells the fry to fish farmers, who look after them until they are large enough to sell to restaurants.

"One day I want to get married and have children, but only boys."

Edgar Flores

"My name is Edgar, but my friends call me 'Gar Gar'. Before school I open about 300 oysters, then another 200 when I get home. I like helping my parents with the oysters, because it means they have enough money to send me to school. I want to do well at school because then, when I am older, I will be able to earn money to give to my mother for buying rice. When I grow up, I want to be a carpenter. I would build a big boat to take people to Guimaras, the island where we used to live. It has mountains and caves, and you can pick fruit off the trees there."

Tem-Tem   Edgar   Ta Ta

Nonoy

EDGAR'S FRIENDS
These are Edgar's friends Tem-Tem, Ta Ta, and Nonoy. They like playing hide-and-seek together. Ta Ta is Edgar's best friend.

"I would like to live on Guimaras again. The houses where we live now are so crowded, and the river is too dirty to swim in. Rubbish should be thrown in a bin, not just anywhere."

This is Edgar's social studies lesson. The writing says: "I am a Filipino. My country is the Philippines."

EDGAR'S SCHOOL
Edgar walks the short distance to the village school. His favourite subject is social studies, in which he learns all about the Philippines. He also learns maths and English. Edgar and his family speak Pilipino, which is the national language of the Philippines.

Oysters and rice

"I wear these clothes most of the time. I like my green top because when it rains, I can pull the hood over my head."

EDGAR'S MEALS
For breakfast, Edgar eats noodles and bread. For supper, the family usually has leftover oysters that are too small to sell. They eat rice with the oysters, and sometimes fried fish, which is Edgar's favourite food. Edgar loves the smell of frying fish.

"This is my pet chicken. I used to have a dog called Blackie, but he disappeared. When I was five years old, I was bitten by a dog, and now I am scared of barking dogs. The other thing that scares me is lightning, because it might strike me. During the rains, we sometimes have typhoons. Once, after a terrible storm, we had to rebuild our house."

TOYS AND FIRECRACKERS
Edgar made this truck himself, using tin cans and old flip-flops. At Christmas the older boys set off firecrackers, which are fireworks that make a loud bang. Edgar thinks that firecrackers are the most exciting things in the world.

Subaedah

SUBAEDAH DAENG NGONA lives with her family on the island of Sulawesi in Indonesia. She isn't sure how old she is, but thinks she is probably ten. Subaedah lives in a village called Polongbangkeng Selatan. Her father is a buffalo farmer, and her mother makes clay pots and ornaments to sell. Subaedah's family belongs to the Makassar people, who come from the southern part of Sulawesi. The Makassar have their own language and customs.

"My little sister, Kamaria, is six years old."

A HOUSE ON STILTS

Subaedah has lived in this house all of her life, and says that she likes everything about it. The house is built of wood and, like most houses on the island, it stands on stilts. Eight people live in the house. They are Subaedah, her mother, father, uncle, sisters, and brother. Subaedah likes to sleep on the floor, which she finds comfortable. Her mother uses the downstairs part of the house as a workshop for making her pots.

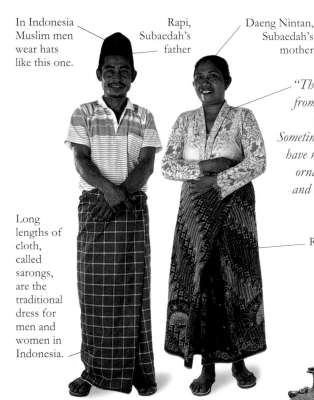

In Indonesia Muslim men wear hats like this one.

Rapi, Subaedah's father

Daeng Nintan, Subaedah's mother

Long lengths of cloth, called sarongs, are the traditional dress for men and women in Indonesia.

"This is Ma. She makes pots from soft clay, then she bakes them until they are hard. Sometimes she makes clay cats. I have never tried to make a clay ornament. It is very difficult, and it takes a long time. One day I would like to try."

Rapi and Daeng Nintan's loose, cool, sarongs are ideal for Sulawesi's hot, sticky climate.

Halijah

Rabina

This clay vase was made by Subaedah's mother.

Daeng Nintan has decorated the vase with a dragon design.

HELPING MA

Subaedah calls her parents "Ma" and "Bapa". Every day Subaedah helps her mother with the chores. She gets up early to sweep the house, then she and other children from the village go to collect firewood before school starts. She walks a long way to find wood, then cuts it with a knife and carries it home. Collecting the wood takes her about two hours. Subaedah thinks it is hard work.

SUBAEDAH'S SISTERS

Subaedah's older sisters are called Rabina and Halijah. Rabina is 15 years old, and Halijah is 12 years old. Subaedah also has a little sister, Kamaria. Subaedah says that she never argues with her sisters.

Beautiful hibiscus flowers grow in Subaedah's village.

RICE PADDIES

Subaedah eats rice with most of her meals. Rice grows in hot countries that have plenty of rain. It is cultivated all over Asia, in special flooded fields called paddies. This rice paddy is near to Subaedah's village.

"Ma has put special oil in my hair to make it look shiny and pretty. I don't like it to look shiny, because my friends might make fun of me."

Subaedah's name is pronounced *Soo-bye-ay-dah*.

SUBAEDAH

"Subaedah is a long name, so most people just call me 'Soob'. I was named after a miracle well in Mecca, which is the holy city of Islam. When I grow up, I want to be a doctor, because sick people would pay me lots of money to get better and then I'd be rich! I would like to visit America, because there I could see people with hair that is a different colour. Everybody here has black hair. If I could change anything about the world, I would make all the bad people good. Only one thing scares me and that's ghosts, because they might kill me."

"This is my best friend, Yupita. She is kind, and always shares things with me."

Subaedah's school

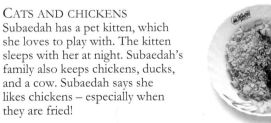

"The worst time of year here is when it is hot and dry. The hot weather makes my skin go dark, and I prefer to have pale skin."

"This is my Bahasa Indonesia lesson. I don't know how to write Makassar. It has a different alphabet to Bahasa Indonesia."

LESSONS AND LANGUAGES
At school Subaedah is learning Bahasa Indonesia, which is Indonesia's national language. At home her family speaks Makassar. Subaedah thinks that the most difficult thing that she learns at school is maths.

"Sometimes when we play, I am naughty – I throw dust at my friends. I love to play, but what I like doing most of all is sleeping!"

Subaedah plays a game called "house" with these little jugs that her mother made for her.

Subaedah hits the top of the tyre with the stick to make it roll along.

FAVOURITE GAMES
Subaedah likes to run along with her tyre and stick. Her other favourite game is *gundasi*, which she plays with stones. She throws one stone up in the air, and tries to pick up as many other stones as she can before catching the first stone again.

Subaedah wears canvas shoes to school, and flip-flops at home. Today she is wearing her best sandals.

CATS AND CHICKENS
Subaedah has a pet kitten, which she loves to play with. The kitten sleeps with her at night. Subaedah's family also keeps chickens, ducks, and a cow. Subaedah says she likes chickens – especially when they are fried!

SUBAEDAH'S MEALS
Subaedah eats mainly rice, corn, eggs, beans, chicken, and potatoes. She doesn't like buffalo meat, because she thinks there is too much fat on it.

Rice, egg, and chicken

Mangoes are Subaedah's favourite food.

Ngawaiata

NGAWAIATA EVANS IS NINE years old and lives in the far north of New Zealand, in a village called Whatuwhiwhi. Ngawaiata's mother is a Maori, and her father's ancestors emigrated to New Zealand from Wales. It is a Maori tradition for children to be brought up by their grandparents, and Ngawaiata, together with two of her cousins, lives with her grandmother in a house by the sea. Many of the people who live in the village are Ngawaiata's relatives. Her parents live in the nearby town of Kaitaia.

NGAWAIATA'S BEACH
Ngawaiata's grandmother's house overlooks this beach, called Whakararo Bay. When Ngawaiata is not at school, she spends most of her time playing here with her cousins. The children play hide-and-seek, using the rocks and trees as hiding places. Sometimes they sleep on the beach at night, snuggling up together under piles of blankets to keep warm. Ngawaiata's father keeps a boat at the beach. He often takes the children fishing with him.

Ngawaiata's grandmother has 24 grandchildren.

NGAWAIATA'S FAMILY
Ngawaiata's father, Philip, works for the local electricity company. Her mother, Norma, is an administrator at an organization that runs Maori language schools. Ngawaiata has a brother, Ben, who is 16 years old, and a sister, Kitingawai, who is 14 years old. They are both away at boarding school, but Ngawaiata sees them during the holidays.

Norma   Philip

"On fine days I often see dolphins in the bay. I climb up my favourite tree and watch them from my lookout post. Sometimes they jump up from the water. We also see them when we go out fishing in the boat. Daddy takes us towards them so that we can get a closer look."

Ngawaiata calls her grandmother "Nanna".

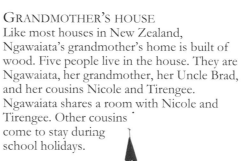

GRANDMOTHER'S HOUSE
Like most houses in New Zealand, Ngawaiata's grandmother's home is built of wood. Five people live in the house. They are Ngawaiata, her grandmother, her Uncle Brad, and her cousins Nicole and Tirengee. Ngawaiata shares a room with Nicole and Tirengee. Other cousins come to stay during school holidays.

THE BEACH HOUSE
Ngawaiata's parents stay in this beach house when they visit Whakararo Bay. When Ngawaiata's grandfather died, he left a piece of his land to each of his children, to be passed on to their children and never to be sold. This makes sure that the land around the bay will always belong to the family.

CHURCH ON SUNDAYS
Ngawaiata is an Anglican, which means that she follows the Christian religion of the Church of England. She goes to this church on Sundays with her grandmother and cousins.

THE CLIMBING TREE
This is the tree that Ngawaiata loves to climb. At night the children sometimes play "spotlight", which is hide-and-seek in the dark with torches. Ngawaiata often hides in the tree.

NORTHLAND
These are the hills around Whatuwhiwhi. The climate in this region, called Northland, is very mild, and the landscape is green, with gently rolling hills.

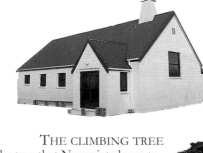

Ngawaiata.

"My hair used to be very long – I could sit on the tips. I had it cut this year; it had heaps of split ends. The hairdresser gave the hair to Mum, and now it's in the cupboard."

"Ngawaiata is the Maori word for psalms. My family usually calls me 'Bab', which is short for Baby, as I am the smallest. I came to live with Nanna because I am half Maori, and I wanted to find out about that part of me. New Zealand is a nice place to live, and I love it here by the beach. In a town you can't do very much, but here I am never bored. I can go walkabout, play on the rocks, climb the trees, or go for a swim. When I grow up, I want to be a nurse, because then I could help my Mum, Dad, and Nanna if they became sick."

"I'm afraid of big dogs, because they might attack me with their sharp teeth. I'm scared of possums, too, because they have big claws."

Ngawaiata

GREENSTONE KURU
This pendant, called a *kuru*, belongs to Ngawaiata's grandmother. She lets Ngawaiata wear the *kuru* on special occasions. It is made of greenstone, a type of jade found in New Zealand.

"During the school holidays, many of my cousins come to stay at Whatuwhiwhi. I don't know exactly how many are here at the moment, but it's heaps!"

LEARNING MAORI
Ngawaiata's school (right) is run by one of her aunts. The lessons are taught in Maori, and the children learn about Maori history and culture. The Maoris were the first people to live in New Zealand. They arrived there about 1,000 years ago, sailing from other Pacific islands in great ocean-going canoes.

Ngawaiata has been writing in Maori in her school book. Maori uses the same alphabet as English, but some letters, such as S, are not used. "Wh" in Maori is pronounced "F", so Whatuwhiwhi is pronounced *Fatufifi*.

"I like reading and studying Maori. We also do maths, and that kind of thing. At the moment we are reading this book, about a man who tries to catch the sun to stop it from going down. I haven't finished it yet, so I don't know what happens at the end."

Ko Maui me te Rā

FOOD FROM THE SEA
Ngawaiata and her relatives eat lots of fish, which they catch in the bay. On the beach they collect shellfish and seaweed. Ngawaiata doesn't like eating mussels, because she thinks they have a bitter taste. She also dislikes pumpkins, except when they are made into pumpkin soup.

"The weather here is usually warm, so I wear shorts most of the time. If it gets cold at night, I put an electric blanket on my bed."

"If I could wish for anything, it would be for a big house next to my favourite tree."

This type of fish is called a John Dory. Ngawaiata catches fish using a line and bait.

Shellfish from the bay

Mussel fritter

Scones

Rosita

ROSITA IS EIGHT YEARS OLD and lives in Western Australia. Rosita is an Aboriginal Australian. The Aboriginal people were Australia's first inhabitants, and they have lived there for more than 40,000 years. Rosita's family lives in an Aboriginal community called Bidyadanga. People from five different Aboriginal groups live in Bidyadanga, and they each speak their own language, as well as English. Rosita's family belongs to the Nyangumarta people.

Rosita's little brother, Dion

BARBEQUE AT THE BEACH
Bidyadanga is near to the coast, and Rosita often goes to the beach with her mother and grandmother. There they cook fish, which Rosita catches with a rod and line. Rosita searches for wood to make a fire, then, when the wood has burned, they cook the fish over the hot coals. With the fish they eat damper, a traditional Australian bread made from flour and water.

ROSITA'S HOME
There are four rooms in Rosita's home. Rosita sleeps in the same room as her mother, grandmother, and her brother, Dion. Her cousins Shannon, Sharon, and Leroy sleep in another room, in bunk beds. Rosita's mother does the cooking outside the house on a wood fire. Rosita helps her mother by getting the plates and cups ready before meals.

Carol, Rosita's mother

Rosita's grandmother

Rosita calls Carol "Mummy".

THE BUSH
This is the road that leads to Bidyadanga. The community is 182 km (113 miles) from the nearest large town, which is called Broome. Australians call the countryside "the bush". Out in the bush there are huge cattle stations that each cover thousands of square kilometres. Around Bidyadanga, small trees and grasses grow in the red, sandy soil. The Aborigines know which wild plants and roots to eat.

ROSITA'S FAMILY
Rosita lives with her grandmother, mother, and little brother, Dion, who is five years old. Her father is away in another part of Australia. Rosita's mother is a cook in a take-away food shop. In Aboriginal communities, people often take care of each other's children, treating them like members of their own family. Rosita calls many of her friends "cousins".

"Sometimes when we play hide-and-seek, I climb up a tree and hide in the branches."

Rosita likes drawing and colouring. She has drawn this picture to show you what Bidyadanga looks like.

"We have a television here, but I don't like watching it. I prefer playing outside."

Rosita's shorts and T-shirt are cool to wear when the weather is hot. In winter, Rosita wears a track suit and jumper.

Rosita

"When I grow up, I want to work in an office, counting the money. I would like to visit Perth, a big city south of here. My teacher, Miss Mitchell, went there and has told us all about it. I wish it didn't have tall buildings though, because small children might fall out of them. If I could change the world in any way, I would make all the tall buildings small."

Jessica

Carla

"When Miss Mitchell went to Perth, she bought me this pencil case with my name on the front."

ROSITA

ROSITA'S FRIENDS
These are Rosita's friends Jessica and Carla. Their favourite games are hide-and-seek and basketball.

TIME FOR SCHOOL
At about eight o'clock in the morning, the school bell rings to let the children know that it is time for school. Rosita likes reading, drawing, and doing sums. She eats her lunch at school, and her favourite school meal is hot dogs.

Rosita's school

Rosita's writing book

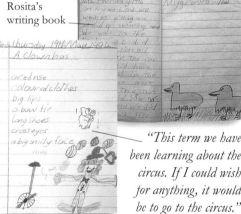

"This term we have been learning about the circus. If I could wish for anything, it would be to go to the circus."

SCARY SHARKS AND SCUTTLING CRABS
Rosita's favourite animals are the penguins and seals that live around the coast of Western Australia. Rosita also likes chasing crabs on the beach. She tries to catch them in her hands as they scuttle quickly across the sand. Rosita is scared of the sharks that live in the sea nearby. Once a group of sharks swam under the boat that she was sailing in.

"Sometimes we have terrible cyclones here. They wreck the trees, and we have to stay indoors until the storm has passed."

TUCKER
Australians often call their food "tucker", and food that they find and eat out in the bush is "bush tucker". Rosita and her family dig up bulbs, called bush onions, to eat. They also eat *wangala*, a type of lizard, and birds that they call bush turkeys. At home, Rosita's favourite meals are chicken soup and egg on toast.

"I don't wear shoes – I haven't got any. None of the children here wears shoes. Sometimes I step on things and hurt my feet, but not often."

Gabiny fruits grow on trees around Bidyadanga.

Damper bread

Bush onion

Our travel diary

"BARNABAS AND I VISITED 31 countries to make *Children Just Like Me*. In most cases, UNICEF arranged for us to meet a child and his or her family. We carried everything we needed to set up a photography studio in each child's home, including four large lamps, nine tripods, and four cameras. This enormous amount of equipment weighed 110 kg (242 lb). Before the fun of the photography sessions began, I chatted to each child, getting to know them well. I found out about their family and friends, their school time and play time, and what made each child special. So Barnabas knew just what to photograph. On our travels, which took us more than a year, we had many memorable experiences..."

"Celina, from the Amazonian rainforest in Brazil, tells me all about her life in the village, her family and friends, and what she does at school."

"Celina has told me that she always sleeps in a hammock."

"The interview is over, and the next day Barnabas photographs Celina and her friends and family. Most of the people in the village turn up to watch."

"The interview and photography are over, and Barnabas and I are paddled back across the river in a leaky canoe."

"Omar helps Barnabas to photograph his snorkelling gear."

March '94, India

NO ELECTRICITY
"OUR PHOTOGRAPHIC LIGHTS NEED quite a lot of electricity. On the construction site in New Delhi, India, where we photographed Meena, we arrived to find no electricity. We were told that the power would return, but after waiting for four hours we gave up hope and photographed Meena outside. One of the things we realized through our travels is how fortunate we are to always have electricity and running water where we live."

April '94, Ethiopia

MOVED TO TEARS
"ONE OF THE MOST MOVING moments in our travels was meeting Abebech Gobena, who founded and runs the orphanage that we visited in Ethiopia. Seeing how much love and care she gives to Tadesse and all the children who live in her orphanage brought Barnabas and I to tears!"

July '94, Thailand

A TALE FROM THAILAND
"SOMETIMES WE HAD TO REMIND ourselves that our gestures might not be appropriate in some countries. I often found it difficult to stop myself hugging the children with whom we had made friends. As I went to cuddle Suchart, the Thai novice monk, he leaped away from me. Thai monks are not allowed to get that close to a woman! However, Suchart loved the photography, and he helped Barnabas at every opportunity."

"Trouble ahead as we take to the road in Bolivia."

"Meeting Bogna and her family."

"Barnabas photographs Erdene in front of his *ger* in Mongolia."

"In Indonesia, Subaedah and I get to know each other."

"Children in Thailand gather round for a photography session."

"In Poland, Bogna's sister Zofia tries out Barnabas' camera."

July '94, Vietnam

TROPICAL TROUBLES

"THE WEATHER HASN'T ALWAYS BEEN on our side. In Vietnam, we had to drive Thi Liên and her family from her home to our hotel several kilometres away, because we needed to use the hotel's electricity supply. While Thi Liên was away, torrential tropical rains washed away all the roads to her home. Even our four-wheel drive car could not get through, and the family had to spend the night in the nearby village. Thi Liên was happy that her journey ended early. This was her first time in a car, and it made her feel very sick!"

September '94, Brazil

AMAZONIAN ADVENTURE

"OUR 110 KG [242 LB] OF photographic equipment was often a burden, but especially when we had to carry it across a river filled with piranha fish and alligators, in a leaky canoe. During our visit to Celina's village, we danced the tribe's special dances with them, and we bathed with Celina in her river. At night we slept in hammocks in Celina's house, listening to the sounds of the crickets, and the dogs howling outside."

October '94, Mexico

MEXICAN MEMORIES

"BY THE TIME WE REACHED Mexico, our tape recorder was not recording properly. But it still played cassettes, so we gave it to Omar. He was so touched that he wanted to offer us a gift, too. He ran off, returning with five of his most precious toy cars in his hand, and we had no choice but to take one, so as not to offend him. Barnabas and I tried our best to choose the one which he would miss the least."

November '94, Far East

MARE'S MILK AND SCORPIONS

"WE WILL NOT forget some of the unusual foods set before us in the Far East. These included deep-fried scorpions in China, and one-year-old fermented mare's milk, placed before us as a great honour, when we visited Erdene in Mongolia."

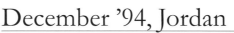

December '94, Jordan

NO NOMADS

"WE VERY MUCH WANTED TO include nomads (people who move from place to place) in this book, so UNICEF arranged for us to photograph a nomadic child from a Bedouin family in Jordan. However, there was a heavy snowfall in the area just before we arrived, and the family had simply packed up and disappeared without trace."

January '95, Lapland

TWILIGHT TIMES

"PHOTOGRAPHY IN LAPLAND in late January is not easy. It only gets light – a sort of twilight – for about two hours every day. Just a few weeks earlier, and it would have been dark all day long! The child we photographed, Ari, gave me his reindeer boots, which he had grown out of and which fitted me perfectly. They were just the thing to keep my feet warm in the freezing temperatures. Barnabas was so jealous that he bought himself a pair, too!"

January '95, Poland

CHEERING UP MEENA

"BY THE TIME WE MET BOGNA, in Poland, we had already been on several trips, so we had some pages of *Children Just Like Me* to show the children. When Bogna read the pages about Meena, who lives in India, she thought that she sounded sad, so she wanted to send some of her toys to Meena, to cheer her up."

February '95, Canada

STICKING TOGETHER

"WHILE MAKING *Children Just Like Me* we experienced just about every type of weather there is, including tropical storms, desert heat, and torrential rain. In the remote Northwest Territories of Canada, where the Inuit people live, the temperature dropped to -38°C [-36°F]. It was so cold that Barnabas' beard froze, and my eyelashes froze together so that I couldn't open my eyes!"

"Our little friend Lydia, from the Maasai tribe in Tanzania."

"Barnabas photographs a *maniva* root in Brazil."

"In Bolivia, this 13-seater plane waits to fly us from Camiri to Santa Cruz."

"Listening to Guo Shuang in Beijing, China."

Index

Acknowledgments

Barnabas and Anabel would like to thank:
All the children and their parents who participated in the book; all the staff at UNICEF, particularly Robert Smith; the UNICEF National Committees and Field Offices in the countries we visited and the people working with them, especially: Gaye Phillips (Australia); Gema Báez, Alan Court, José Soto (Bolivia); Sheila Tacon, An Snoeks (Botswana); Angela Alvarez Matheus, Christèle Angeneau, Karin Hulshof, Agop Kayayan (Brazil); Lisa Wolff (Canada); Farid Rahman (China); Amel Gamal (Egypt); Mark Thomas (Ethiopia); Gisèle Chaboz (France); Ilias Liberis, Kiriakos Vassilomanolakis (Greece); Edit Kecskeméti (Hungary); Anthony Kennedy, Madé Sutama, Rihana Bakri (Indonesia); Avraham Lavine, Ruth Ogdan (Israel); Kazushi Matsuda (Japan); Jalal Al Azzeh (Jordan); Mario Acha, Rafael Enriquez, Jorge Jara, Norma Salazar Rivera and DIF, (Mexico); Katherine Hinton, (Mongolia); Sergio Soro (Morocco); Tim Sutton (New Zealand); Keshab Mathema, "Butz", Tin Tin (Philippines); Malgorzata Mularczyk (Poland); Park Dong-Eun, Park Soon (S. Korea); Rozanne Chorlton, Mr. Mawi (Tanzania); Norbert Engel (Thailand); June Kunugi (Vietnam).

Thanks also to: Abebech Gobena Orphanage; All China Women's Federation (Wang Wei); DK Inc (Nancy Lieberman, Mary-Ann Lynch, Jeanette Mall); DK Moscow (Elena Konovalova); Darlington School, Sydney; Dong Fang Primary School, China; Éditorial Atlantida (Veronica and Alfredo Vercelli, Marisa Tonezzer, the Pereyra Iraola family); Okalik Eegeesiak; Helsinki Media (Helena Raulos); Sari Inkinen; Jubilee School, Jordan; Kendriya Vidyalaya School, Delhi; Kiryat Anavim Kibbutz, Jerusalem; Maori Women's Welfare League (Areta Koopu); Narayanan; National Native News, Alaska (D'Anne Hamilton); National Centre for Children, Mongolia (Sunjidmaa Altankhuyag); Nev e Shalom (The Peace School), Jerusalem (Coral Aron); Shobita Punja, Bikram Grewal, Brinda Singh, and the Mobile Crèche, Delhi; Alison Pritchard and La Grange School, Western Australia; Pukinmäki Elementary School, Helsinki; Prema Rajan; Fabienne Reverdit; Russian Classical Dance School, Moscow; St. Michael's Montessori School (NYC); Shinnam Primary School, Korea; Helena Svojsikova, DK; Peter Tamakloe; Vallaeys School, Blaye; Waitangirua Intermediate School, Wellington.

Dorling Kindersley would also like to thank:
Christiane Gunzi for editorial advice; Jane Parker for the index; Shalini Dewan and Vicky Haeri at UNICEF in New York.
Additional photographs
The publisher would like to thank the following for their kind permission to reproduce the photographs
tl – top left , tc – top centre, tr – top right, cla – centre left above, ca – centre above, cra – centre right above, cl – centre left, c – centre, cr – centre right, clb – centre left below, cb – centre below, cbr – centre below right, bl – bottom left, bc – bottom centre, br – bottom right
Michael Copsey 10cla, 10cl, 11tr, 49cl, 56tl, 56cra, 67tr
Robert Harding Picture Library Scott B. Smith 16tl, Robert Frerck 11tl, cla, Richard Ashworth 26cl, Tony Waltham 26c, Robert Francis 26cr, 27cla, Christopher Rennie 27tr, 49cra, Mohamed Amin 49cr, 67cl
The Hutchison Library Errington 37cla, c
Pictor 27tl, c
Still Pictures 36tl, Edward Parker 36cr
Tony Stone Images Colin Prior 10cra, Tom Till 11c, Ary Diesendruck 11cr, Nicholas Parfitt 37c, cra, Nicholas Devore 48cl, Robert Everts 48cr, 49cla, Daniel J. Cox 66cl, Robin Smith 66c, Jerry Alexander 66cr, David Austen 67tl, David Hiser 67ca, Paul Chesley 67cr
World Pictures 10cl
Every effort has been made to trace the copyright holders. Dorling Kindersley apologizes for any unintentional omissions and would be pleased in such cases to add an acknowledgment in future editions.